LEADERSHIP RECRUITING

CONSULTING SKILLS
FOR RECRUITERS

SIMON MULLINS + KELLI VUKELIC

DEDICATION

This book is dedicated to all recruiters.

Ours is not only an honorable and valuable profession but also a critical one for all organizations, whether public or private, small or large, for-profit, not-for-profit, or governmental. No entity is successful without people, and we are literally the gatekeepers of the future of the organization, whether we deal with executives or recent graduates. As such, we have an immeasurable role to play in both the success of those organizations as well as on the lives of the people that we interact with every day.

LEADERSHIP RECRUITING
Consulting Skills for Recruiters

Copyright ® 2022 LDRS Publishing, Inc.
www.LDRSPublishing.com

ISBN: 978-0-578-93402-0
Library of Congress Control Number: 2021913870

Printed in the United States of America.

Edited by: Monica Jainschigg
Design and Production: Jayme Johnson, Worthy Marketing Group
Book Development and Marketing: Carolyn Monaco, Monaco Associates

CONTENTS
● ● ●

1.

INTRODUCTION
• • •

I n our experience, very little content is created with the "recruiter-as-consultant" in mind. Much is written on sourcing skills, evaluation, or leadership assessment, but there's not much out there on how to actually interact with candidates and clients. Yet, this consultative part of the work is what truly differentiates good recruiters from the rest, and from the latest trend in artificial intelligence. Some would say that this consultative part of the role will be the last piece remaining once the robots have taken over; we haven't seen that movie yet, but perhaps it's coming soon to a theater near you.

The idea for this book came from a collaboration between the authors in the middle of an incredibly volatile time in the world. Kelli had recently left her role leading a strategic function at the largest global executive search firm; given this experience, coupled with the research that she had done for her master's degree in industrial and organizational psychology, we saw an opportunity to co-design a professional development curriculum on consulting skills for recruiters, which is still available online. However, after completing that project, we realized that even more needed to be done to remedy the gaping hole in the relevant content. From there, the content blossomed into this book.

This is actually the second book in our Leadership Recruiting series, with the first one focused on strategy, tactics, and tools for hiring organizations. Like the first, this is as much a textbook as anything else, and also like the first, it is not a page-*turner* but a page-*stopper*. Much of what it contains is not new material, and it's certainly not rocket science. It's more of a compilation of others' brilliant research on topics such as emotional intelligence, empathy, and the journey to being a trusted advisor. What *is* new is that we have tailored these ideas toward the recruiting function and, hopefully, made them more consumable and usable, whether you are part of an in-house recruiting team or in a consulting firm. We have added our own commentary to the theories, based on decades of experience both recruiting directly as well as managing teams of recruiters globally. Perhaps more importantly, however, we have been fortunate enough to have some outstanding recruiting leaders and practitioners share their personal perspectives and anecdotes. Not only do these stories add excellent context to the theoretical concepts and bring them to vivid life, but they also show that great recruiting consulting skills are essentially the same, regardless of region, industry, or what side of the table you sit on. We are very grateful to these contributors for spending time on this project and sharing their insights, experiences, and wisdom with us.

After having studied this space in the course of our own work, and in creating professional development content that focuses on the leadership recruiting space, the one takeaway about the journey to becoming a trusted advisor (which is what this book is really about) is that it is always a journey, and not a destination. It is unlikely that you will read some tips and tricks and be able to master them the next day. Becoming a trusted advisor will take time and practice—and mistakes—but the tools, techniques, and ideas presented in this book will support you on that journey.

As always, we welcome your comments and insights as we continue to advance best practices to a point where the most important hiring decisions are made with the greatest opportunity for success.

2

STARTING WITH THE BASICS
• • •

We use a simple framework to describe the executive search process, using the "3 Ds" of Definition, Discovery, and Decision. Recruiters will use their consulting skills throughout the entire process, but perhaps most consequentially at the Definition stage. Before we get into the more strategic aspects of consulting skills for recruiters, we need to make sure we're all on the same page when it comes to the basics.

The Search Process - D³

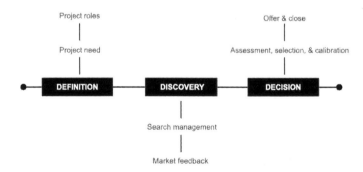

This would include a core set of tools for every client meeting to ensure that both consultants and clients are getting the most value from the interaction. Also, as we discuss consulting work in this book—whether it is internal/in-house recruiting or work on behalf of an external recruiting firm—we use the word "client" to describe the hiring decision maker. Some in the corporate world might be more comfortable with the term "hiring manager," but for the purposes of this book, they are the same.

PREPARE FOR THE MEETING

The first of the core tools we want to address is the basic kickoff meeting framework, including the meeting setup. It may sound obvious to some, but you need to make sure you have enough time allocated to gather all the information you need from the meeting, whatever the agenda. You also need to make sure you're going to be in front of the right people, the ones who will give you the information you'll need to deliver the best value for the client. Again, it might seem obvious, but in our more timid days, the authors of this book might have agreed to a 15-minute search kickoff meeting because the client was "too busy" to give us more time. Or we might have agreed to meet with the chief of staff or HR business partner "who's handling this for me" because "they know what we need." No, they probably don't. And even if they do, they are not the final decision maker for those make-or-break questions. For that matter, the client might not know the answer either, but at least they are on record as having made a statement to that effect! In our experience, searches run around 50% longer if the client is not directly involved at the outset and throughout the engagement.

Much of what we discuss in this book comes down to "owning your space" in the room when consulting with the client. It is very easy to feel "lesser than" a very senior executive who manages thousands of people and makes millions in compensation. But while you should undoubtedly show respect for their seniority and position and for what it took to them to get where they are, it is critically important that you also respect your own expertise. In addition, you should honor that client's decision: They could have chosen any number of consultants to talk to about this search, but they put their trust in you. You and your team owe it to that decision maker to bring your whole self and deliver the best service based on your skills and your experience. Remember, also, that people generally defer to experts, so make sure that you establish your expertise before you get too far into the meeting. In the search firm world, you might have brought out a list of some of your completed searches in an earlier "sales" meeting, but it's worth referencing again, albeit briefly. In the corporate world, mention a few recent hires into the organization (ideally successful ones!) to ensure they realize that you do this level of work all the time and to differentiate yourself if the client is new to leadership-level hiring practices.

One thing we cannot stress enough about any client meeting is the need for preparation and premeeting research. Even if it's the very first meeting and you have scant information about the search, you can at least make some good assumptions based on the title of the role, the title of the person you are meeting, and the business group they work in. Furthermore, you can hazard a guess about the experience that the client has in hiring at this level, and if you're part of an in-house team, you can probably do much better than guess, thanks to your own records. You can also discover the reputation of the leader or the group you'll be dealing with. Naturally, be careful not to make too many assumptions or early decisions based on this prework; otherwise, they might derail the conversation. However, the preparation will likely set you up for a much higher-value meeting when you actually walk in the door, and a much better plan when you walk out. Plus, if you discover that the client is new to this level of hiring, then it will both help guide the meeting, especially if you have to coach the hiring team somewhat, and help you cover all the bases with them so there are no surprises later. Some people advocate for sending a few high-level questions to the client before the meeting so that they can start thinking in the direction that you want them to—not so onerous that they become "homework" and certainly not the same questions as you will ask in the room, but enough to get everyone on the same page. Finally, in preparation, be current. Has the hiring manager recently done an interview or has a podcast? What have they said on social media recently? Do your homework too!

GATHER INFORMATION IN THE MEETING

One useful tool is a checklist for the actual meeting. This might include pointers to make sure you understand why the role is open and what happened to the prior incumbent (because you know candidates will want to know!). If it is a new role, then you'll need to discover what has changed in the business to create it. Additionally, if it is a completely "greenfield" role (i.e., one where the new hire has to make everything up as they go), you'll also have to find out what buffers and protection will be built in to ensure the new hire doesn't fall off the rails. This conversation checklist should also include bullets about expectation setting around roles and responsibilities, and—critically—time frames. You may have to tell the client it will take three times longer to fill the position than they first thought, especially if they've never hired at this level before. That won't be an easy conversation, but better to have that it now than one-third of the way down the "You must be kidding!" timeline!

One of the best tools available to a recruiter is the consultative questioning framework. Originally designed to assist salespeople, it is now often used for all types of consultative engagements and is exactly the right fit for recruitment consulting. Saying that, the model should be used carefully, as it can come across as interrogative—and even potentially irritating—if you drill those questions down to the nth degree. When you use this framework, you should monitor both yourself and the person you are engaging very carefully. You and your team are in the room to be learners and consultants, and not interrogators.

Though we will mostly discuss using this methodology with clients, it should be noted that consultative questioning can be used with candidates too. With candidates, and particularly "prospects" who are not yet candidates, it is important to understand their motivation before you start "selling" the opportunity. We always say that you have to put coat hooks on the wall before you can hang up your coat. In other words, find out what makes the prospect tick and then afterward, tailor your message to those responses.

Much of how we approach these consultative conversations will be covered in depth in the rest of this book, especially when we talk about empathy and listening skills; for the moment, we will share some actual example questions and phrases you can use.

It is important to clarify key terms at the beginning with questions like: "Thank you for that overview. When you say _____, what does that mean to you in this context?"

The answers will often lead to more questions, and from there, you will be asking mostly "how" and "what" questions. It is best to avoid what are called "leading questions"—those that encourage the "right" answer—as you're all about learning in this context and not winning agreement.

Some consultative questions that are more specific to recruiting include:

- "What business problem will this new hire be solving?"
- "What are some of the actions you would expect the new hire to take in the first six months?"
- "What are your top five selection criteria for candidates for this search?"

- "What are the top five criteria for success for this new hire?"
- "How will the new hire be measured in a year?"
- "What are the main things the new hire will be doing to solve the XYZ problem?"
- "Why was the last person in the role not successful?" or "The last person in the role was promoted to a more senior position—what was it that made them so successful?"
- "What will happen if you don't hire this person?"
- "What do you see as the next career step for this person, after they have proven successful in this role?"

Here are some useful qualifiers to help you drill down on whatever you need to:

- "So, you mentioned…"
- "I'm curious. Why…?"
- "What do you mean by…?"
- "Let me see if I understand you. Are you saying that…?"

And this is a particular favorite of ours if you can't get a clear or specific answer from the client:

- "I know you said you don't know the answer to that question, but could you share your best guess/share what comes to mind/imagine what some possibilities might be?"

In some situations, it's best to let the client run through a complete overview of the situation and what's important to them before you ask any questions—you don't want to break the flow or miss anything that they might share in their stream of consciousness. Plus, if you try and pin them down on specifics too early, you might end up going into depth on something that is not that important to the search. Just be sure to take careful notes while they are talking. Afterward, you can go back and summarize what you heard. Asking if you missed anything often triggers more information. Then you can drill down on what are the most important points, clarify any selection criteria, and most crucially, rank those criteria in importance to the search and the hire's success. If you hear that "all the criteria are important," then perhaps ask how the client might choose between two candidates, one with more of X criteria and one with more of Y criteria, all else being equal. It might help!

Given that so many leadership candidates are less interested in the compensation and benefits and so much more interested in the impact of the role, it's important that you come out of this kickoff meeting with the "why" of the role. You need to know: What is its purpose? What will the impact of the role and the new hire be? How will they be able to change the product line, the business, the market, and so on? This is what really turns the head of leaders when they are so close to the top of Maslow's hierarchy of needs (i.e., the study of how humans are motivated).

SET UP A COMMUNICATION SCHEDULE

One key outcome of that initial meeting has to be an agreed communication schedule. As we've mentioned, a disengaged client makes for a frustratingly long search, so we strongly recommend creating regular update meetings—ideally at least every two weeks—and ensuring that the client joins them. These meetings need only be around 30 minutes or less in the early days, and even though there might be little to update in certain periods, just checking in and perhaps sharing feedback from the market or "heard on the street" news is likely of value.

We have heard some people say that the best day of any search is the day the project starts, and it rapidly goes downhill from there. We would say that's a little cynical, but any tactic we can use to keep engagement high is certainly a good thing. In this vein, we have heard of some recruitment teams that have a regular segment of their updates focused on general competitor or market news, as opposed to sharing only what is happening on the search. If you do this, limit this information to only a couple of bullet points—after all, at the end of the day, you're there to deliver a hire for an open role. But if you can add more value than expected and assist with the client's business agenda, all the better. It is our belief that recruiting organizations know, store, and sit on more useful business information than they realize; it wouldn't take much to package that information into value-added, strategic nuggets of useful data for your business leaders. You should also emphasize that the information you're sharing is scarce and exclusive to them and their search, which will give it even more value in their eyes. They will thank you for helping them look good in front of their boss at the next strategy meeting!

To help prepare the hiring manager and interview team for how long the search will take, as well as clarify each of their roles in the process, we recommend using a timeline and roles/responsibilities framework.

Who Does What: Recruitment Process

1. Plan ▶ **2. Source** ▶ **3. Screen** ▶ **4. Select** ▶ **5. Hire** ▶ **6. Contribute**

PREPARE
- Role opens
- Organization assigns the engagement to the executive recruiting/search team (in-house/external/both)
- Preliminary research/prepare for client briefing

ORGANIZATION BRIEFING
- Initial briefing meeting
- Additional stakeholder meetings identified
- Meetings held
- Confirm sourcing strategy

SOURCE
- Execute sourcing strategy

SCREEN
- Resume reviews
- Initial phone interview

PRESENT
- Prepare candidate report
- Present candidate report to Hiring Manager
- Prepare candidate and Hiring Manager for interview
- Manage candidate(s) through the interview process

CLIENT OVERVIEW
- Candidate interviewed by client
- Discuss interview outcome
- Conduct additional interviews with HR and other stakeholders as necessary

SELECTION
- Decision is made to approve/decline candidate
- Notify candidate(s) of outcome
- Conduct behavioral or psychometric assessment
- Review assessment results

OFFER
- Confirm offer package to be extended
- Extend verbal offer and confirm acceptance
- Initiate and review pre-hire background checks
- Extend written offer

PLACEMENT
- Collect candidate's written acceptance

POST HIRE
- Submit employee experience survey per company standards
- Follow up with both parties at regular intervals

— Human Resources   ⋯⋯⋯ Hiring Manager   ⋯⋯⋯ Executive Search Team   Candidate

CRAFT A ROLE DESCRIPTION

After you have prepared brilliantly and collated all the data from your various conversations, the most important output is a role description. It is our belief that this is often a wasted opportunity. It's easy to grab a few similar role descriptions and cut and paste, to just throw a few things together. But a good role description can be used in a better way – as a form of contract for the project you're about to move forward on. It should clearly explain the key criteria for the successful candidate from the point of view of the ideal experience, skills, or competencies of the person you're looking for. It should also state what success looks like for the candidate once they've been in the role for at least a year. Having a document like this, created after your discussions with the hiring team and then approved by them, means you are essentially crafting a statement of terms for the project: What you're looking for, what success looks like, what the expectations for the candidate are, and so on. You can then refer back to it as the project goes on, and it might be useful as a reference point if the client decides to change direction halfway through the search, if only to clarify that the strategy has changed. It also helps to tell the story to the talent that you are approaching, and it becomes a marketing document as you source your candidate networks. In fact, having things clearly written out in this way often triggers people to remember others whose backgrounds resemble the requirements laid out in the document.

Insist on a Clear Role Description

- Time spent clarifying the role description raises the hiring manager's engagement and shortens the search.
- The role description should focus on specific outcomes expected of this role in the upcoming year.
- A well-crafted role description aligns internal stakeholders and saves time later.
- The "Top 5 Criteria" should be clearly evident in the role description.

DEFINE THE PARAMETERS

There is some debate as to whether you should enter the kickoff meeting with researched names and biographies that you've unearthed based on what little you know of the search so far. This might go awry if you have things wrong and can thus diminish the hiring manager's confidence in your understanding or capability. Whether or not to introduce this research depends on the strength of your "trusted advisor" skills as a recruiter. If it's clear that the research is for guidance and calibration only and to help define the prospect pool, and you're confident you can own that conversation, then it can be extremely helpful. In other circumstances, this kind of work might be better kept for a second meeting. Whenever you choose to have this conversation, it is again as much an exercise in calibrating the exact search parameters for the recruiter and zeroing in on what the hiring manager is truly seeking.

It's often helpful to categorize the research and biographies into three buckets or lists and guide the hiring manager through them, specifically validating what is written in the role description. The first, or "core," list likely includes all the usual suspects – those who seem an obvious match for the role. If this is a particularly short list, it could help start the conversation about how restrictive the hiring manager's criteria are. The second, or "close," list might include prospects who do not meet all the criteria or who may have comparable alternative skills and experiences. This can help drive the conversation toward the option of a broader target candidate pool or, better yet, a more diverse one. The third, or "creative," list will test the boundaries of the search and potentially open the hiring manager's eyes even further. If this list includes people whom you believe are not even remotely likely to be hired, you can explore that unlikelihood and its reasons with the hiring manager. It's an opportunity to question assumptions, such as: "People from company X would never answer our calls," which could be because the hiring manager or team have grown used to not calling them!

In the same conversation, your team and the client's team might talk about "no-go" organizations. This can be an opportunity for you to push back if the reasons are nonspecific or arbitrary. For example: "I used to work with someone from company XYZ, and they were terrible, so don't bring me anyone from that company." It's worth testing whether this "no-go" is actually about the culture of that organization or just an interaction with one person, as your prospect pool can rise and fall dramatically based on this determination.

THE THREE LISTS

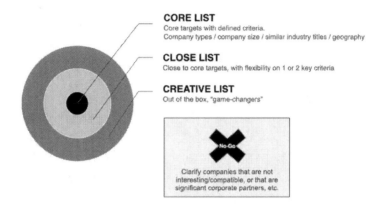

CORE LIST
Core targets with defined criteria.
Company types / company size / similar industry titles / geography

CLOSE LIST
Close to core targets, with flexibility on 1 or 2 key criteria

CREATIVE LIST
Out of the box, "game-changers"

No-Go

Clarify companies that are not interesting/compatible, or that are significant corporate partners, etc.

One key capability in the recruiter's toolkit, which you will find comes up in various chapters in this book, is the proper use of data. As stated above, it is important to get a good set of data at the outset and use it to show an understanding of the direction of the search. We also talk about using data to help the client understand the talent landscape and explain how the search is going in chapter 10 ("The Trusted Advisor"). And since not all searches go smoothly, you can also use data to help redirect a search that is going off-track. Perhaps it's taking a surprisingly long time to close, or the client is complaining that you're not doing the job well. When a search is in trouble, what next? First, gather data—which is always the best place to go. Communication is often the issue in troubled searches, including failure to set proper expectations at the outset. So, we recommend that you pull together a document that shows the original search parameters, including the top five criteria. Include a complete list of prospects researched and contacted, then a metric of those who responded and the reasons they were rejected or not interested.

This kind of thorough research will impress a frustrated client. Stark and unfiltered feedback from prospects—especially those who seemed a good match on paper—also helps reset the direction of the search and the client's expectations. While this feedback should not be a surprise at this point, seeing it as one report can be striking. Not only does a periodic summary give comfort to the client that you are actually working hard on their behalf, it also gives a reality check on the challenges of the search, and possibly the role itself. Never assume that the client is taking all your communications about an engagement and reviewing it in a consolidated way before every meeting or update. Transparency into the search will further support the development of your relationship and build trust with the client, putting you on the same side of the table if the engagement becomes more challenging later on.

One other basic tool that is always available to you—which costs nothing but is perhaps the hardest to use—is the word "no." As much as you may want to help every client and ask "How high?" when they say "Jump!" it is sometimes the wrong thing to do as you build your credibility—especially if you are building a relationship or a new executive recruiting function. As your reputation grows stronger, clients often want you to work on more of their searches. That's flattering, but sometimes these new projects are at a lower tier than your remit. Or they might be out of your specialist area, or perhaps you don't have the capacity to carry out the quality of work that created your reputation in the first place. It's natural to want to say "yes," but you should always consider if it is better in the long run to turn the project down or send the client to an alternative provider. It might not feel good in the short term, but it is likely that it will be rewarded in the long term.

For further reading, we recommend:

Leadership Recruiting: Strategy, Tactics and Tools for Hiring Organizations, by Simon Mullins and David Lord (LDRS Publishing Inc., November 2, 2020)

LEADERS' WISDOM:
USE DATA TO IMPROVE DIVERSITY PIPELINES

• • •

This is an example related to using talent intelligence and data to change the direction of an executive search strategy. It also shows how you can effectively manage and steer client expectations. The problem here lies in the fact that as a beverage bottler, we are a commercially driven organization. Our executive leadership career path is very much based on a solid career in sales. It is critical to have such a background. At the same time, we have a big push on hiring diverse talent, which in many regions our company operates in means increasing the number of female leaders. Unfortunately, there is a big drought of female sales leaders in our industry, with significantly more marketing profiles. Hence, we were struggling to bring a good and diverse shortlist to the client in our searches.

To address the issue, my research colleague and I took a close look at the top management team composition of all the major FMCG companies. We measured how many females were on the board of directors and in the executive leadership ranks and also investigated their functional career progression. We combined this research with our own real-time, day-to-day intelligence from direct sourcing and interviewing. As a result, we observed that the vast majority of female general managers and senior executives in FMCG come from a marketing commercial background, then jumped into general management. So for a company like ours, which is highly sales-driven, it would be very difficult to find a direct match with what the client was looking for. We shared the insights coming from this research with our Executive Leadership Team sponsor, enabling us to push for a more flexible approach to the requirements of our commercial leader searches and the targets and segments of where candidates should come from. Thanks to this integrated data-driven effort, we changed perceptions and were able to build broader pipelines with more female talent.

—Juan Calvo, Group Talent Movement and Executive Search Manager, and Christian Henning, Talent Consultant, Coca-Cola HBC

3.

EFFECTIVE STAKEHOLDER INTERVIEWS
• • •

To *deliver* more than expected, you need to know more than expected at the outset of your search. Stakeholder interviews are very valuable research tools for kick-starting a recruitment process and understanding the business. Charles Kettering, an American inventor, engineer, and business leader, was the head of research at General Motors and is famously quoted as saying "a problem well-stated is a problem half-solved." In this chapter, we will explore who the stakeholder is, the setup of stakeholder interviews, understanding the business drivers, and exploring light bulb questions.

Who is a stakeholder?

In an executive search process, stakeholders are people in the client's organization who touch the role in some way, including anyone who will influence the outcome of the recruitment process. Interviews with stakeholders are one-on-one conversations about a specific role, and they provide a quality overview of the stakeholder's opinion about the specific role and what is required for the candidate to be successful. Such interviews help you establish the foundation for any search by providing valuable insights that would otherwise be difficult, even impossible, to obtain. These insights will define business goals, technical constraints, usability problems, and many other aspects of the role. You need to plan properly and execute these interviews well. Also, you might be surprised at how differently each stakeholder sees the situation. Analyzing these different perspectives will help you better understand what stakeholders want and need from the future candidate while helping you set successful drivers for them (we'll discuss this below). Once you collect the information, you'll be better equipped to deliver results for your client and eventually better equip the person you hire.

SETTING UP SUCCESSFUL STAKEHOLDER INTERVIEWS

First, select stakeholders to meet with. If you're an insider, you already have a good idea who the influential stakeholders are. But even then, asking the client who the stakeholders are can be quite revealing. You may think that interviewing all of them isn't necessary, but we recommend avoiding this trap. Hearing an influential person's point of view on the ideal candidate filtered through someone else's words isn't the same as hearing the thoughts in their own words. Unfortunately, it has been our experience that interviewers on the team can have strikingly different views of what the successful candidate looks like, or what the role actually entails. This can happen even when the interviewer is on the same team as the client. Even worse, we have seen the client and their boss have differing views of what they are looking for. Best to get these kinds of wrinkles ironed out before the candidates uncover them in their interviews!

Second, understand their roles. Understanding each stakeholder's role in the process and their ability to influence its direction is key. Be clear on the role of each person and their interests in the recruitment. They could be an influencer to a decision maker or an influencer over the direction of the search. Or, just as importantly, they could be an influencer on the success of the eventual hire.

Third, prioritize. Prioritize meetings with decision makers, top influencers, and people who have vital information.

Fourth, meet them face-to-face. In every situation, try to conduct as many meetings as possible in person. Not only is it easier to develop a rapport, but it also gives stakeholders a chance to assess your credibility, which is important for you and your long-term growth as a recruiting consultant. Similarly, as you ask questions and probe discrepancies, you will be able to perceive visual clues that might signal for you to dig deeper in certain areas. Be aware of "invisible" stakeholders, also known as "torpedoes," who can sneak up at a high speed and blow the search out of the water. This kind of unseen stakeholder is usually someone who has the ear of the client and throws their opinion into the mix well after the search has started. For instance, they might step in and offer advice on candidate résumés without having been included in the process since day one and therefore have no context. This can derail the client from the original candidate specification or change their direction entirely, especially if the timeline is extended and the process is taking longer than expected. Always, always ask if any key influencers are not on the original list.

UNDERSTANDING THE BUSINESS DRIVERS

Earning Trust

Showing stakeholders that their opinion matters will not only give you good data to work with, but it will also earn their trust.

Defining Goals

Get a clearer idea about the scope and parameters by speaking to multiple stakeholders.

Sharing a Cohesive Vision

Speak with more than one stakeholder will stop you from second-guessing your recruiting decisions later.

Improving Communication

Talking to stakeholders is the perfect opportunity to really get to know the people working behind the scenes.

Stakeholder interviews help you understand the business drivers behind the recruitment requirements, and there are several other benefits, such as earning the trust of the stakeholders and the client. Showing stakeholders that their opinion matters not only gives you good data, but you'll always find it easier working with people who feel that their voice is being heard during a recruitment process. There's much to learn here—you just have to be willing to listen and take notes. Engaging stakeholders will help you articulate to candidates the key priorities for the role, the business drivers for the role, and how the role fits into the strategic workforce plan. Multiple stakeholder interviews will give you a clear idea about the scope, parameters, and context to help you articulate to candidates the goals, milestones, and tasks they'll need to prioritize once they start in the role. In addition, speaking with more than one stakeholder will help you confirm and support the client's recruitment decision later on and help stop others in the organization from second-guessing the hiring decision. Involving stakeholders is also the perfect opportunity to really get to know the people behind the scenes, and collaboration and good rapport with them will also give you a better sense of and appreciation for the individuals whom the candidate will be working with, allowing you to better articulate that throughout the process.

This is an important time in the process to address stakeholders' competing interests or different priorities to ensure that everyone's expectations can be acknowledged and addressed. Asking everyone the same questions will help you identify themes and focus on emerging solutions, features, or problems.

THE SIX "LIGHT BULB" QUESTIONS

During the stakeholder interviews, we recommend you use these six consistent "light bulb" questions:

What is your role in relationship to this position?

How do you, personally, define success for this hire in 12 months time?

Define your working style with superiors, peers, and subordinates.

What pitfalls should candidates be aware of?

What qualities would you like to see the successful candidate bring?

Is there anyone I need to speak with who isn't on my list? Who?

Once you have completed the interview, read back their answers to the stakeholder. This will likely trigger some further thoughts and input from them and also clarify your interpretation. In addition, you can ask follow-up questions such as:

- "I thought the role would deal with this [class of customers or group of people]. Am I right?"
- "I thought if the role had these goals, it would make it easier to do X. Do you agree?"
- "I put down X as your answer to this question. Do I have that right? Or do I need to add something else?"

Good preparation is the key to successful stakeholder interviews, just like painting a room—it can take as much time prepping the corners and edges as actually painting the walls but makes for a much better finish in the end. Furthermore, while you will have developed some questions in advance, be prepared to let the interview flow on its own. There will be a natural rhythm to the conversation, and you should follow it. As you exchange ideas, dig deeper than the role description. Be genuinely curious, ask lots of questions, and actively listen to each stakeholder's concern. However, be prepared for and aware of inconsistencies between different stakeholders' views. When you debrief the client, point out these inconsistencies and focus on solutions, features, or problems you've identified and work on finding alignment.

Finally, even if your client says that there are no stakeholders to interview, push a little harder. Bear in mind that the exposure you get in face-to-face interactions with these business leaders will help you build your credibility and reputation in the organization—don't be the invisible recruiter behind the scenes. These are opportunities for you to gain internal exposure, and you should take them as long as they will add value to the process.

For further reading, we recommend:

Consulting on the Inside: A Practical Guide for Internal Consultants, 2nd edition, by Beverly Scott and B. Kim Barnes (Association for Talent Development, March 16, 2011). See especially Section II: "The Consulting Process," Section 7: "Information and Assessment," pages 77–92.

LEADERS' WISDOM:
STEPS TOWARD BEING A TRUSTED ADVISOR

• • •

One of the first things that's important to being a trusted advisor or consultant is you just have to have credibility, and that can come in a lot of forms. Some things just take time, though sometimes you can build credibility very quickly with a client on a first interaction. Sometimes it's about you and your team's "brand," or reputation. Plus, you have to deliver: Do what you say you're going to do. Clear communication in articulating your processes and deliverables is important, as well as organization skills. Again, do what you say you're going to do, with strong follow-up. You also have to know the business and the marketplace. That comes with time, but it also comes with hard work and research. Just like a lot of good business development people do, in recruiting you're going to research your clients and try to understand the business, the individual, and the team. Understand where there may be soft spots or opportunities to sell candidates on; plus, understand what their dilemma may be. You want to try to think like the business. Though you are a talent advisor, there's a lot of business questions, like, "What are you really solving for?" It's good to assess your hiring managers too: Are they more junior? Is this the first time hiring at this level? Will you have to manage or coach them a little? Also, what is the business group's brand in the external marketplace? What is the impact of that brand on the talent market?

It's important to ask yourself: Are you a good advisor? Are you balanced? Do you have the right intentions? As they are the client and the hiring manager, you don't want things to be confrontational, but you also want to make sure you direct things properly and consult on their decisions. You know the opportunity and the talent and can help make sure the client is not too narrow in their thought. You give them options. You challenge them a little bit in their thinking by asking good probing questions and make sure they're thinking about things the right way, especially in the diversity and inclusion space, where we encourage our hiring managers to cast a wide net on diverse slates and candidates: What is tied to this role? What are you trying to solve for? Where are you going? What impact does this role have? Not just in the operations, but in the broader organization and the team. Sometimes you're lucky to get the bare bones of the facts of the search in the intake meeting, so these might have to be follow-up questions, whether in writing or in person.

—Dan Connolly, Vice President, Executive Search Practice Leader, Comcast

4

EXECUTIVE COACHING
• • •

E xecutive coaching has been used to enhance skills and improve performance in a wide range of organizational settings. Coaching is probably one of the most—if not the most—individually tailored practices in talent development, as it involves a close and confidential relationship between the coach and the person being coached. Though we might not label it as such, a recruiter is often coaching their clients and candidates, and recognizing how this can impact and improve the results of an executive search is very important. John Whitmore, author of *Coaching for Performance*, sums it up thus: "Coaching is unlocking people's potential to maximize their own performance. It is helping them to learn rather than teaching them." This chapter will talk about the informal coaching role; the "everything coach"; striking a balance; what coaching is not; and ethics and impact.

HOW DO RECRUITERS ACT AS COACHES?

Your role as an informal coach to candidates and clients can be invaluable to any and every process. Coaching is an informal relationship between two people of whom one has more experience and expertise and offers guidance, while the other person learns. Consider this definition from your perspective as a recruiter—all the times you have informally coached in a recruitment process. Now let's start with those experiences and enhance your perspective and approach.

Experienced recruiters play the role of informal coach more often than they realize. They provide a safe, structured, and trustworthy environment in which to offer support. Recruiters also help others understand their current competencies and how they're perceived by others. The best executive coaches possess conversational intelligence and can actively listen to business leaders, focus on what they're saying without interruption, then respond thoughtfully. They are teachers rather than lecturers. Additionally, your clients will likely have a lot to learn as they journey through the hiring process, especially if they are new to it or to the level or function being hired.

Both internal and external coaches can be found offering different levels of support, and recruiters can play all of these coaching roles informally every day:

Career coaching: A career coach provides support for individuals looking to make a career transition, whether short or long term, including guidance on professional development, résumé writing, online profiles, and interviewing. Recruiters are often in the position of guiding candidates on their career choices, sometimes toward the organization, and sometimes away from it.

Life coaching: A life coach supports all aspects of life, including career, finances, and family—a role often played by recruiters in the offer negotiation process.

Organizational coaching: An organizational coach supports leaders in identifying goals, creating strategies to obtain these goals, and boosting the overall performance of the organization or team. This is a role that senior recruiters often play in more sophisticated organizations as they guide their hiring managers through the senior hiring process.

Performance coaching: A performance coach supports those within an organization who need to improve their work performance. This type of work often comes into play as a result of a performance appraisal process, regardless of level or job title, and is a role senior recruiters might play to junior recruiters on the team. As more and more organizations are beginning to have their in-house executive recruiting organizations also manage internal talent movement, this type of coaching is likely to become more prevalent moving forward.

In the role of recruiter and consultant, you should seek to be a reflective practitioner and strike a balance in your coaching style that seeks to hit a medium point between observing and telling (*advocacy*) and observing and asking (*inquiry*).

Advocacy lets you help other people see what you see and understand your thinking by giving examples to describe your perception of the other's reasoning. Advocacy helps you see negative consequences of another's actions and provides a way to point them out without suggesting that they intended those consequences. Advocacy helps you disclose your emotions in a way that does not imply that the other person is responsible for creating your emotional reactions.

In contrast, inquiry helps you find how others see the situation by asking them for examples to explain their thinking. You can use inquiry to encourage others to identify possible gaps or errors in their thinking. Inquiry helps to seek out another's views of a situation and can be expanded on to uncover what leads the person to act or choose as they do. Inquiry also allows you to discern other people's emotions. It offers a safe space for people to ask others for help and to tease out whether or not they are a contributing factor to the problem.

In a leadership recruiting role, we practice both advocacy and inquiry throughout the process: We use inquiry in understanding and interviewing the candidate as well as working with the client to elicit the requirements of the role. We then advocate for the candidate with the client and also advocate on behalf of the hiring team as we come to closure with the candidate.

A lot of people confuse coaching with counseling or mentoring. Coaching is different from these practices in several ways.

Counseling is defined as a professional guidance of the individual by utilizing psychological methods, especially in collecting history, conducting a personal interview, and testing. While coaching may involve a hefty amount of introspection, it does not offer therapeutic outcomes. In counseling, that introspection largely involves looking toward one's past, whereas coaching is future-oriented.

Mentoring is a self-directed, mutually beneficial, long-term relationship between two individuals for long-term career movement where the mentor does most of the talking and offers advice. It most typically consists of a more experienced person directly guiding the mentee through the experience that the mentor has already been through.

As a recruiter, you probably already lead every day with a conscious commitment to always do the right thing. Although your role is not a formal coaching relationship, at times it interacts with confidential and sensitive information about people and organizations, and you must operate within the same ethical guidelines that guide personal communications and the boundaries established by your organization and your client. You may often be called to help others in making a close call on ethical matters, and your ability to project a consistent set of values and stay steady through ethical issues will help to make you a trusted advisor to many. Keep in mind:

Confidentiality: Always maintain the strictest levels of confidentiality.

Responsibility: Act within the bounds of your qualifications, competencies, expertise, training, and certifications.

Professionalism: Make sure all your verbal and written statements are true and accurate.

Society: Be responsible to society, maintaining fairness and equality in all activities and operations while respecting local rules and cultural practices. This includes, but is not limited to, discrimination on the basis of age, race, gender expression, sexual orientation, religion, national origin, disability, or military status.

In general, you must act honestly, with compassion, respect, and dependability. A recruiter who breaches organizational trust and inappropriately handles sensitive information harms their team, their organization, the client, and the profession. We remember one situation where we were in a quandary as to what to do with certain information that had been shared with us, and how we should use that information moving forward with our candidate. At the time, we were given superb advice by one of our colleagues: *Think about how you would feel if you were asked to explain your course of action in front of the board of directors. Would you feel comfortable with that conversation or not?* In the course of the leadership recruiter's work, you are often privy to very sensitive data, and that single question might well help to keep you—and any recruiter—on the right path.

YOUR IMPACT AS A COACH

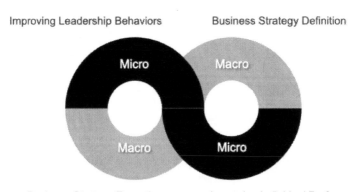

Improving Leadership Behaviors   Business Strategy Definition

Micro   Macro

Macro   Micro

Business Strategy Execution   Improving Individual Performance

Executive coaching has been used to enhance skills and improve performance in a wide range of organizational settings. Coaching has a larger impact on micro-level outcomes, such as improving leadership behavior and individual performance, than on macro-level outcomes, such as business strategy, definition, and execution. Recruiters are uniquely positioned to enable candidates to realize their potential and achieve breakthroughs in a new role. The one-on-one relationship built during the recruitment process, along with the data collected through interviews and references, can provide an experience that is tailored to individual values, strengths, core organizational purpose, motivation, capabilities, and experiences. The outcome of this orchestrated scenario is a motivated executive learner who joins the organization, recognizes their own development needs, and is then fully supported by the organization in their motivation to act and change. Your role as a recruiter in this process can make a significant impact: Don't miss the opportunity to play the role.

An oft-neglected space where coaching comes in very useful is with clients. Many assume that our senior clients are omniscient and all-powerful, and came out of the womb with fully formed leadership abilities. Well, that might not actually be the case, though they might not share this fact too openly. As part of your "owning your space," you need to find a way to discover how experienced the clients are at senior-level interviewing, assessing, and hiring. And remember – you are very possibly more experienced than they are. This discovery might have to be done sensitively, as we've sometimes found that some serious egos can come into play at this level. However, it is highly likely that even the most senior leaders will be happy for some coaching on how to do this—if only to make sure they stay within the law.

We've also found that the most-needed space for client or interviewer coaching is when we are working on opportunistic hiring or long-term external succession planning projects (or ESPs, as we call them). It seems that the lack of a role description and/or résumé can really throw some leaders off their game, so they often need coaching on how to approach prospects, how to network with them while finding out salient facts, and how to think about these prospects for the long term.

Now, how do you take away everything you've read here and practice it in your organization? Here are some suggestions:

1. Be a sounding board. The best executive coaches possess conversational intelligence and can actively listen to people. Focus on what people are saying without interrupting them and then respond thoughtfully. You have a unique perspective, one that people can get only from someone with years of experience.

2. Impart your fundamental understanding of the business. Use your knowledge and experience to offer candidates the chance to explore issues that may be holding them back in the process. Listen to a problem, tell people what you've seen in the past that has worked or hasn't worked, and discuss different ways the problem could be solved. You can't make decisions for people, just as sports coaches can't substitute into a game for an athlete, but you can guide them toward better decision-making.

3. Provide a confidential space. The old axiom "It's lonely at the top" rings true for many. Sometimes people aren't comfortable sharing their issues with others, believing that their problems are too unique for others to understand or too private to divulge. Like executive coaches, recruiters can give business leaders and candidates a private, confidential space to talk about the challenges they often mull over alone. Help people see that others have experienced similar issues; allow them to get out of their heads and look at the issues with a fresh perspective.

4. Teach from real-world experience. Experience is a powerful teacher, and there are few better ways to learn than seeing if what you've tried before succeeds or fails. You likely have volumes of stories that you have learned as a recruiter. Use them to help people avoid some of the same failures.

5. Help set goals and hold people accountable. You have the opportunity within your teams to help people set goals and tie those back to what's best for the organization.

6. Finally, commit to lifelong learning. What do Bill Gates (Microsoft), Elon Musk (PayPal, Tesla), and Warren Buffett (Berkshire Hathaway) have in common? Aside from their wealth and years of success, they're all committed to reading and continuously learning. Much like these hugely successful leaders, the best executive coaches never stop learning. So read, study, and speak with other people who are knowledgeable so you can stay on top of your game. Being externally curious about business will help you become a more valuable source of information and wisdom in your role as recruiter as consultant and coach.

For further reading, we recommend:

Executive Coaching: Practices and Perspectives, 1st edition, by Catherine Fitzgerald and Jennifer Garvey Berger (Davies-Black Publishing, 2002)

LEADERS' WISDOM:
SOMETIMES YOU HAVE TO BREAK GLASS FOR THE GREATER GOOD

● ● ●

There was a situation a few years ago with a senior female leader who was very happy at her current company and a very passive candidate. I had interacted with her several times in my network, and finally there was an opportunity and the timing was right, though it was very opportunistic. I reached out, she agreed to talk, and we fell in love with her. We got to an offer stage and she turned us down, saying it was too risky to leave such a stable position. The hiring manager almost took it personally and was very disappointed and even a little bit angry about it. However, I totally went to bat for this person because I really believed in her and walked him off the ledge. I counseled him, saying I still believed in the candidate and that I thought he still believed in her too, and that maybe we should see it through her eyes and go back to her with more assurance and an even bigger commitment. He and I collaborated on next steps for the candidate and afterward, I went back to the candidate and persuaded her to have an informal chat with our hiring manager in a location other than our office about the company's value proposition and her career. Between us, we salvaged the deal, and she's still with the bank and is a particularly successful story doing great things. The key here is to take the emotion out of it, make it more of a business conversation, and look at it from the candidate's point of view. I also think you need to be humble. Everyone has an ego, but I just come at people as a very down-to-earth, real person. I like to use comments and phrases like, "If you think that this opportunity is a healthy opportunity for you and your family... ," as it's not about winning or getting a bigger bonus; it's about being sincere. I will ask the candidate, "Do you think this is the right fit for you—is it going to support your career aspirations?"

I've had another situation where we were talking about a candidate and we were really close to making this person an offer. However, I had to say to the hiring manager, "Let me share with you some more recent observations and red flags I now have about this person," and I gave her my very real feedback.

I felt we could close this job with this person, but I thought we could find someone who'd ultimately be a better fit. That wasn't what the hiring manager wanted to hear. She wanted to close the job, and she was at a point where she had other things to do and wanted to be on the other side of it. I think a lot of people probably would have just gone with that, but I would lose sleep over it, because I don't really then have my client's back. The hiring manager followed my feedback and, in the end, when we backed out, the candidate didn't take it very well and got really aggressive. Afterward, the hiring manager said, "Thank you—I think we dodged a bullet there." Sometimes it's not always a popular decision we have to make, but I think the clients trust me to have their best interests at heart, and that's really important.

—Scott Stearns, Director, Recruitment Manager, Talent Acquisition and Staffing, MUFG

5

CONSULTING SKILLS
• • •

Consultants bring their expertise to identify organizational problems, support the analysis of those problems, and recommend solutions. This chapter will discuss your role as a consultant as well as ideas on how to structure open dialogue, work with feedback, and deal with resistance. A popular adage—and one that well describes the role—is, "A consultant, to be worth their salt, must give honest judgments, not necessarily those that they think the client would like to hear." This chapter will explore the role of the internal and external consultant, traits and skills, common problems, and derailers.

As a recruiter, you often play the role of consultant. As such, you are provided with some tribal knowledge and have an appreciation of the cultural nuances and people systems in the organization that can be considered in making change. Your cultural understanding is not to be underestimated in implementing solutions that require change. And, if you are an internal consultant, you'll have the opportunity to see the long-term benefits of the work you do inside the organization.

Recruiters often support change management in organizations, and this includes specific solutions and sometimes project managing the recommended change initiatives. These initiatives usually revolve around process improvement, but are not limited to that; for example, they can also include process management. Internal consultants can often be found focusing on implementation and continuous improvement, and there are vestiges of this work in a recruiter's role. For instance, the continuous refinement of an organization's recruiting strategy is often left to them, and they can stay invested in following up post-implementation, given their relationship with clients.

Internal consulting can be more organic and ambiguous in nature than external consulting, which is more process-related in its approach, given the milestones that are contractually attached to payment. Often an internal recruiter doesn't even realize they are serving as an internal consultant, but in situations where you see you are acting as one, you should ensure that you demonstrate the traits of a great consultant.

THE QUALITIES OF A GREAT CONSULTANT

A lot of qualities go into making a successful consultant, but the following five are essential to succeed on the highest level:

Professionalism: Consultants should always just keep in mind that the client relationship should remain at a professional level. It's sometimes easy for internal consultants to take an "employee" attitude. But in many environments, this can backfire because you're not seen as outside of the problem that you were trying to solve. In fact, some organizations find they are paying external consultants not only to give the same advice as the internal consultant, but for a halo effect – an impression of greater authority created simply by the fact they have an outsider's view: In other words, a view that is believed to be more objective.

Team player: Consultants must demonstrate that they're team players and are willing to learn, genuinely valuing the input and expertise of others. It's important to establish a collaborative relationship with peers.

Judgment: Consultants are required to have good judgment when confronted with a problem and not jump to conclusions. They should take time to consider the facts and get feedback from peers and management before reaching a decision.

Good communication skills: Consultants should have excellent oral and written communication skills. Since you're often viewed as the subject matter expert, you should be able to communicate your opinions effectively.

Good listening skills: During a consulting process, consultants will meet different people with unique characteristics. You will, too. Make sure you have excellent listening skills and encourage all to talk freely around you. This leads to more information sharing, which in the end can make the recruiting process more streamlined and effective.

Firm grasp of responsibilities: It's important for internal consultants to understand the responsibilities of their role, as well as its practices and parameters.

You may notice that each client has a different take on what the role of a consultant entails. Clarifying your client's expectations and deliverables beforehand may possibly be the single most important task a recruiter as consultant undertakes.

ESSENTIAL CONSULTING SKILLS

Now that we've looked at the traits of some of the great consultants, let's look at the most valued consulting skills and how they relate to the recruiting world:

Creative thinking: Creativity is a top priority in many fields. While many industries may not seem likely to prioritize creative thinking, the definition is broader than you might expect. Creative thinking gives people ideas that go beyond the normally accepted ways of approaching the business of any industry. It encourages brainstorming and listening to ideas from all kinds of people. In a leadership recruiting context, we see this skill being particularly useful when thinking about how to target certain talent pools or how to broaden the pool, especially in looking for underrepresented talent.

Conceptual and practical thinking: Conceptual thinking suggests that you are a visionary and innovative. You may have a strong sense of intuition or the ability to coax ideas from people who have a difficult time finding the words for abstract concepts. You might ask provocative questions in a group brainstorming session to help others think conceptionally and formulate inspirational touchstones for the company you're working for. Once you've established your vision, your practical thinking skills will allow you to help others transform that vision into actionable items and deliverables. You may help outline a specific strategy that narrows a business focus. You can help them organize projects into component parts and assign tasks based on broad ideas that have been customized for the organization.

This skill, in the recruiting world, comes up in a number of ways. It can be how you help the client see what they are really looking for in the role, or how you help them crystallize their thoughts into an actual role description. Similarly, it might be used in translating the business's need into a talent research strategy.

Problem solving: Your role as a recruiter often involves problem solving, possibly without a great deal of advance information on some of the issues you're presented with. Your ability to listen carefully to the concerns of others and react quickly, and to thoughtfully propose solutions, may be among the most valuable skills you can possess. Though it's obvious that you need this skill—because you are there to solve business problems through identifying talented new leaders for your client—it should be noted that it also comes up in conversations with prospects and candidates. How often do you have to pivot in a candidate conversation in response to an unforeseen challenge or newly revealed motivation and readjust your framework?

Clear and empathetic communication: Once you have a solution for a problem, everyone will value your ability to communicate your ideas clearly, concisely, and with empathy. We often quote the experience of writing what were (in our minds) exceptional, thoughtful, and well-reasoned treatises on candidates, articulating multiple important questions at the end, only to realize the client was reading only the first three lines! We can't emphasize "clearly and concisely" enough—keep it to a few bullets and ask critical questions, or impart the most important data up front.

Collaboration with all job levels: As an internal or external consultant, you will need a sense of confidence when working with the stakeholders and employees who will carry out the hiring plan. Developing poise, politeness, friendliness, excellent listening skills, and public speaking skills will serve you well in any circumstance. On any one day, you might be dealing with the CEO of a public company at one moment and the building receptionist the next, and you should show the same respect in both conversations. Similarly, in many organizations you will be partnering with your own team members and extended team members (for instance, HR business partners, executive compensation, and relocation teams, if you're internal) as well as a variety of executive leaders. Being adept at working with all, as you own your own space, is a key skill.

Organization and time management: Work with people in advance to prepare an agenda, and be polite but firm in keeping meetings on task and on time. This skill is a key part of leadership recruiting—and, again, part of owning your space or acting like a true consultant on behalf of the business. Another facet of organization is that in our world, spinning multiple plates, or juggling various balls, is all part of the job. In our experience, the best recruiters seem to thrive on it, but not all are great at making sure their partners are kept up to date or that all the plates are getting the right amount of attention. This is definitely a skill that needs to be worked on, especially when you're dealing with the highest levels of an organization and reputation is everything.

Curiosity: Because consultants work with various people, potentially both internally and externally, a sense of curiosity can help you acquire the information you need to do your job well. Curiosity encompasses asking thoughtful and focused questions and then listening sincerely to the answers. It also helps you understand how each business fits with the framework of its industry and the ways in which that business may be innovating. If management seems detached, you may be able to encourage people to explore candidates from different industries from the standpoint of curiosity. Help them form the right questions to ask themselves about competitive practices. Intellectual curiosity is one of those key skills that are absolutely critical for great recruiters to have, though often missed when actually hiring recruiters as it is quite hard to measure. (We talk about it at length in chapter 6, "Intellectual Curiosity.")

Credibility: Your credibility as a consultant is likely to come from your experience in the field and your reputation as someone who's helped find great leaders for other hiring organizations. Beyond those criteria, you can improve your credibility with further education, any available certifications, or your profile on a professional social media site that allows you to outline your skills and experience. Credibility can also come from knowledge of the space you work in, the talent market, and the competition. The more you study these areas, both directly and through candidate conversations, the more credibility you gain. Credibility will also be gained real-time as you use your knowledge and skills interacting with key stakeholders.

As a recruiter, how do you improve your skills day to day? Daily consulting work is a good place to practice. Even just changing your mindset to recognize that you're acting internally as a consultant will help you start to hone the skills you need. If you look critically at your daily interactions, you'll be able to identify areas where you are strong and areas where you could use some help.

HOW TO IMPROVE YOUR SKILLS

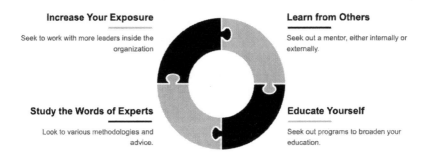

Increase Your Exposure
Seek to work with more leaders inside the organization

Learn from Others
Seek out a mentor, either internally or externally.

Study the Words of Experts
Look to various methodologies and advice.

Educate Yourself
Seek out programs to broaden your education.

Here are some ways to sharpen your skills:

Increase your exposure. Seek to work with more leaders in the organization. Each new experience will give you exposure to something different that can help you expand your knowledge base. You can shape your career through recognizing your greatest strengths. In chapter 3 ("Effective Stakeholder Interviews"), we talked about stakeholder engagement as a way to boost your visibility—this is another opportunity to increase your exposure.

Study the words of experts. Many successful consultants publish scholarly articles, books, and videos that talk about how to develop skills. Find those philosophies and skills, match your professional goals, and study their methods and advice.

Learn from the best. You'll likely be familiar with consultants across many industries, externally and internally, who demonstrate some of the skills you seek to improve. Find out how they acquired their expertise and see if you can find a formal mentor.

Educate yourself. Many professional organizations offer training courses that culminate in certifications. Seek out programs that cover the skills you're most interested in and find out if you can become certified in any or all of them.

As you seek to develop key consulting proficiencies, you can start with some basic cooperation and leadership skills that will help breed trust and positive interactions with your internal clients.

Foster an innovation mindset. Your role as an internal consultant may be to synthesize various ideas and experiences into a new way of conducting business. Your own creative thinking skills may inspire others to share theirs and encourage collaboration and original ideas that the organization can implement.

Collaborate with everyone. Collaboration works well when it's managed by a strong leader, which may be a natural fit for your role in recruitment. A good leader does not dominate a conversation but encourages participation while still guiding the discussion in a focused way, avoiding unnecessary tangents.

Assert yourself. As we've stressed before, as an expert on the topic of recruitment, you should "own" the room. You can validate your position at the table with confidence by asserting your knowledge and demonstrating the professional development you have undertaken.

Be dependable. Follow through on tasks you say you'll do, provide answers when asked, and do the research to come back to the question later if you need to. Meet (and, ideally, overachieve on) your deadlines, and attempt to apply your unique skills in every situation.

DERAILERS

Steven Stowell, Ph.D., of the Center for Management and Organizational Effectiveness, identifies five common problems of organizations, and in our experience, recruiters can come up against them at any time:

1. *Absence of clear direction:* Lack of direction is one of the most common organizational problems, and it stems from two root causes: Too many functions and individuals who lack an understanding of how they fit or why they matter. As a result, people become complacent, content to just show up, take care of the business, and hope that someone in the wheelhouse steers the ship.

2. *Difficulty blending multiple personalities into a cohesive and unified team:* People's personalities vary widely, and the diversity of backgrounds, opinions, views, and experiences can be challenging for teams. This creates a unique set of potential issues and opportunities for you to address.

3. *Failure to develop key competencies and behaviors:* When you work in organizations, you'll encounter a lot of hardworking people. However, despite the good intentions, experience in the industry, technical talent, and subject matter expertise that many leaders bring to the table, creating a high-performance organization is often out of reach. Nearly everyone you meet— including senior leaders—will have at least one, and in some cases, multiple leadership weaknesses. Some of these people are aware of their behavioral shortcomings, but others are blind to their deficits. Compounding this problem is the fact that people inside the organization are often afraid to candidly say what they think. Thus, helping enormously successful leaders address their Achilles' heel can be tricky, particularly in a recruitment process.

4. *Poor communication and feedback:* There seem to be two extremes in this area. Either people do everything in their power to avoid confronting others and holding them accountable, or they relish any opportunity to jump on others' shortcomings, belittle them, and crush their spirits.

5. *Lack of awareness:* Unfortunately, when leaders are busy, focusing on many necessary operational distractions, they take their eye off the teamwork ball. This means that communication suffers, and leaders get preoccupied and fail to recognize people, celebrate progress, build the talent

pipeline, or invest time in reviewing process practices and better ways of working across functions. Team members then become disengaged, feel marginalized, and lose focus and commitment.

As a recruiter, especially if you're working as an internal consultant, you will likely come across other derailers. One of these is low client motivation, usually found in situations where the client isn't initiating the engagement of their own volition. The most common scenario is where a client's boss triggered the recruitment process, and though the client disagrees, they are still pressured to go ahead with the search. Recruiters acting as internal consultants can attempt to overcome this challenge by breaking the engagement down into smaller steps. Accomplishing several small steps in quick succession could create some momentum and provide the client with small wins to begin to feel more motivated to work on the project. Another approach you could use is to develop an effective feedback tool for the client to use with their boss, thereby helping the client look good in their boss's eyes.

Positive communication can help, and it's important to give the client consistent progress updates. As a consultant, part of your role is to give your clients some ownership in the engagement implementation process, effectively giving them some "skin in the game." Often, low client motivation results when the client feels that they have no control over the situation or no say into how it will be accomplished. Most of the ways to overcome this challenge include the recruiter keeping the client in motion. Momentum can be a powerful force that can keep the client moving forward, instead of finding ways to avoid or even stall the process.

Another derailer is resistance, which can be met by recruiters during any phase of the engagement. Resistance is when forward momentum on a project wanes and can show itself as the client being unable to make difficult or unpopular decisions, questioning more than usual, or continually requiring granular detail. While some resistance is natural, you can overcome it by better understanding the motivation behind it. Resistance is often driven by emotion, and it is entirely possible that a topic of greater importance to the client (and which is causing the resistance) has not been disclosed to you. In addressing resistance during consulting engagements, try to identify the types of resistance taking place and discuss it with the client in a neutral way. You can thus pave the way for productive dialogue with the client.

• • •

Change is a fluid process, and while we've shared some steps, skills, and traits, problem solving isn't static and may require tweaks and adjustments along the way. Being open to making slight shifts in your approach as new information comes to light can go a long way in shaping a successful ending. **Decisiveness and leadership are not the same thing.** In leading change, you need to help the client make decisions. And you have to help them model this change in their leadership role. All the cheerleading and rallying around the ideas and process of change cannot substitute for collectively creating a vision that matters, and including all stakeholders. Getting people involved in being part of defining the future is more important than all the fireworks and fanfare that can go around communicating it. It's all about the "why" rather than the "what," which we will talk more about in chapter 8 ("Purpose").

Setting high standards doesn't equal increasing accountability, so focus on creating accountability and connection to the strategy, not having people work down a checklist. Everyone brings competencies to the table, and it's your role to find out what those are and bring them to bear to contribute to change, not to try to fix what you perceive to be broken. Most of what matters in creating change cannot be measured, and your approach internally with clients needs to reflect that. Sometimes you won't see change happening in front of you, so make sure you probe thoughtfully to find it and to celebrate big and small wins. Remember, recruiters have a very significant role in aiding change in organizations as they are literally the gatekeepers of the future leadership of the organization. However, they also walk a fine line between three entities: The client, the organization, and the candidate. It is your job to align these three important entities, even though they may all have a different focus and may define their goals differently. We call this the "Recruiter's Bizarre Life Triangle."

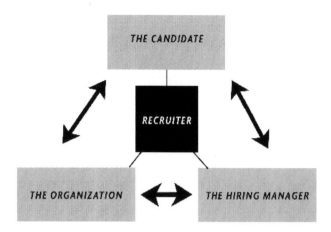

It makes the recruiter's role interesting and at times frustrating, yet we keep coming back because the subtleties and nuances, combined with the "super-secret-squirrel" nature of our work, make it intoxicating—and almost addictive! We get to change the fabric of the organizations we work for and help guide them to their aspiration states. And we do our work largely behind the scenes and unheralded. We are a strange breed living a strange life.

With apologies to everyone, especially to William Wordsworth and Shakespeare, consider the following ode:

I wander lonely as a cloud-based recruiter, never in the circle, always just on the outside—an observer;

I love to watch people, to study them, learn about them, so much so that I became something of a square;

Yet not completely, as I was always close to things ... no, not completely square;

And at the same time, not in the circle, not owning the decisions, just party to them, advising them;

Always watching, studying, questioning, learning, seeing; Yet more than just that—much more than that.

Influencing, guiding, selecting, and sometimes, rejecting.

*In one corner, **I protect my organization and its leadership, its protocols and policies**; though sometimes I break glass, not too much, and always for the greater good;*

*Yet in the same instance, I support my **hiring manager client**, and help move the business forward; I push for decisions, I drive for results, I deliver in a creative fashion.*

I am not afeard, I do not always jump whenever they shout, or ask "How high?" I follow the intent, not always the letter.

*But wait—in another corner I also advocate for **my candidate**, ensuring their success and future, best positioning them to make the greatest impact on the organization, to change the world— while not giving away the farm;*

*Aye, I am always between these three points—**organization, client, candidate**;*

More mystical than a stuffy square;

More points than a smooth circle;

Always on the outside, yet always on the inside, working the three magical points together;

*Balancing the three, sometimes disparate, sometimes together, but always with me at the center: **The Recruiter's Bizarre Life Triangle**.*

For further reading, we recommend:

Consulting on the Inside: A Practical Guide for Internal Consultants, 2nd edition, by Beverly Scott and B. Kim Barnes (Association for Talent Development, 2011)

Flawless Consulting: A Guide to Getting Your Expertise Used, by Peter Block (Pfeiffer, 2011)

LEADERS' WISDOM:
INFLUENCING AND EDUCATING OUR CLIENTS

● ● ●

I think that we need to somehow have a balance between pleasing our customers and, at the same time, letting them see the implications of what they are asking for. And sometimes what they want is not what should be done, so we also need to play that role of being an advisor—a consultant—and let them know the implications of their decision.

This is what happened in a recent example: We were doing a search, and the interim leader came up with a brilliant idea that he wanted his whole leadership team to interview everyone for the position he is covering for. He wanted to put multiple people in front of five different interviewers, which became complicated, with around 40 meetings. Then one of the interviewers also complained to the head of HR and said, "Why do we have to interview eight people?" So we investigated, and apparently the interim manager wanted to show a fair process and wanted everybody to have the same opportunity and to get feedback. But it's a lot of time, so we decided we needed to influence and negotiate and come up with a win-win situation. The process got modified, and they reduced the number of people, but we had to let the interim manager know what could potentially happen if he did this and suggest "Why not try this alternative plan?" He understood it and was OK with the proposed process, but it's constant education and influencing throughout our work.

In a different situation, we had one candidate who was recommended to one of our senior leaders, and no matter what, he wanted to hire that candidate. But the candidate was making it very difficult to recruit, always putting road blocks up and trying to get around our assessment process. They asked, "Why do I need to talk to this person?" or "Why do I need to do the assessment?" and so on. Everything was a challenge in the whole interview process. So we talked to our partners in the business's HR team and involved them. We also involved other business leaders and made them aware of the situation. We kept involving people so that everybody was aware of how complicated it had become. It is our job to give the right people the heads-up, show the red flags of what was coming out in the process, let them know, "If you hire this person, it might not be a good role or company fit," and share what happened when we had similar situations in the past. At the same time, though, you need to consult and you need to put everything on the table. You have to be flexible as well. At the end of the day, it's their decision, but they need to have their decision made with their eyes wide open. And that's our job—to make sure their eyes are open.

—Adriana Quevedo, Head of Executive Search and Onboarding, Intel Corporation

INTELLECTUAL CURIOSITY
• • •

Why is intellectual curiosity important in the role as a recruiter? In 2016, Capital One's then Vice President of Talent Acquisition, Jennifer Anderson, said in *Fortune* magazine (March 3, 2016), "We know we have found a good candidate when we see a deep intellectual curiosity, a passion for our mission and to drive positive change, and an inclination to lead with heart and humanity."

In this chapter, we will explore what intellectual curiosity is, why it is important, how you grow it, how to test for it, and why you need to hire intellectually curious recruiters.

WHAT IS INTELLECTUAL CURIOSITY?

There are a few definitions of the term "intellectual curiosity," and they all touch on aspects of recruiting in some way or another. Intellectual curiosity is curiosity that leads to an acquisition of general knowledge and can include wanting to understand such things as what objects are composed of, underlying mechanisms, systems, mathematical relationships, languages, social norms, and history.

When talking about intellectual curiosity, it's important to bear in mind the difference between *being intellectually curious and being curious about things that do not lead to an acquisition of general knowledge*. We want to consider curiosity that leads to information relevant to the recruitment process. Intellectual curiosity makes your mind active instead of passive, and people who have this trait are those who want to grow. Curious people are always thinking of questions and searching for answers and that's what makes their minds stronger. Our minds are like muscles—the more you use them, the more they develop, and the mental exercise of curiosity is what influences intellectual development. Intellectual curiosity is a key for success because it can support you in your career just as much as any other skill. The barrier to curiosity is self-consciousness—perhaps concern about looking bad, asking foolish questions, or appearing "lesser than" in front of the client. Frankly, these concerns are likely to be all in your head; chances are, the more curious you are in front of the client, and the more you ask value-adding, consultative questions, the more you will both prepare yourself for a more successful search and help your client get clarity on the purpose of the search.

CULTIVATE INTELLECTUAL CURIOSITY

Here are three reasons that explain why intellectual curiosity is important:

- It makes you observant of new ideas. When you're curious about something, your mind is engaged with that subject. It expects and anticipates new ideas that are connected to it. When new ideas appear, your mind is going to recognize them. If you're not intellectually curious, new ideas may pass right by you and you won't see them—or recognize them if you do see them. This happens because your mind isn't prepared or focused to catch them. Just like trying to hail a taxi in London, you'll get nowhere if you don't look out for it—and then it's gone before you realize it.
- Intellectual curiosity opens up new worlds and possibilities; without it, these can't be visible. Everyday situations and regular activities make uncurious minds unable to see what intellectual curiosity enables one to see.
- It brings excitement into your life. Curious people have interesting lives, full of new information, ideas, and infinite things that attract their attention. Everything can look like an adventure to an intellectually curious person.

Here are some ways to develop intellectual curiosity.

- *Keep an open mind.* If you want your mind to be curious, you need to keep it open to find out about new things, to learn, unlearn, and relearn. Being ready to change your mind, to accept new information, to change perspective—these are the main characteristics of an open mind.
- *Don't take things for granted.* Intellectual curiosity and open minds have a general push toward research. To develop intellectual curiosity, it's important to always question things and challenge different opinions. Don't take things for granted, ever. Always dig deeper and try to find out what's hiding under the surface of things and events around you.
- *Ask questions, relentlessly.* Dig deeper to find out more about what surrounds you. It's widely stated that what, why, when, who, where, and how are the best friends of curious people.
- *Don't label something as boring.* If you label in advance, the door of different possibilities is closed. Curious people never call things boring, and intellectual curiosity makes you always see new doors to an exciting new, place. That doesn't mean that there's going to be action toward that new direction immediately. The door stays open in order to be visited another time. If there's no time to explore it right away, your brain won't forget it, and when it sees information related to it again later, the curiosity in you will pick it up and start thinking about it anew.
- *Read diverse kinds of literature.* Instead of focusing on just one type of reading, if you want to develop intellectual curiosity, choose a different book. Read a novel, or a history book, or a biography, or an art book, or a book about science. Choose a new author. And keep going.
- *Consider learning for its own sake.* Have you ever learned anything without being obligated to do so? Intellectual curiosity means that you are seek new things to learn, just to find out more about something—or about something completely new.
- *Embrace the unknown.* People without intellectual curiosity are often afraid of new things, afraid of change, and dedicated to the status quo. To develop intellectual curiosity, it's important to embrace new things, embrace change, and be brave enough to initiate change. "Why?" and "Why not?" are two powerful questions to ask yourself and challenge your

intellectual curiosity. Practice this for every single thought and see the conclusions you make.

WHY HIRE INTELLECTUALLY CURIOUS RECRUITERS?

We believe heads of executive recruiting or talent acquisition should look for intellectually curious recruiters because, first, they learn faster. These people are always thinking and absorbing new information, and they are precious once you find them. Also, they fight the status quo and are always challenging old solutions, finding a better way to do something—and they won't stop until they find it. They think it can always be done better, smarter, faster, and are not afraid of change. At the same time, they play well with others. Employees with well-developed intellectual curiosity are usually good at working within teams. They're always asking questions, reaching for solutions, looking for different opportunities to help and solve problems. Finally, they bring in knowledge. Inside and out of the business, these people are genuinely open-minded, and because of that, they never stop learning and finding out about new things and ideas. A large body of knowledge will enter your organization in this way.

How do you test for intellectual curiosity? A great way to determine whether someone is curious is to seek out clues during an interview. Ask the curiosity question. For example, ask, "Tell me something you've taught yourself in the last six months." Or, "How did you go about teaching yourself this new skill or idea? What was the result?" You can also ask if the candidate has a question for you: If you get a boilerplate response from an internet source, they're probably not the person you're looking for. If you get a question that's creative or original in some way, then this is the one you want. You're trying to find out about a candidate's "fixed" or "growth" mindset. Ask about mistakes they've made and how they learned from them. Ask questions like "Tell me about a time when you had to complete a project but weren't given all the details." How much or how little context they provide will be a good indicator of their level of curiosity. Scenario-based questions also give candidates the opportunity to show if they're naturally driven to ask questions or dive deeper into how a particular process works. Ask them how they do their research when they want to learn about something they know little or nothing about. Ask other questions like: "What books have you read lately?"; "How do you learn new things?"; "How do you strive for self-improvement?"; "Are you self-taught in any skill?"; "What interests you the most about this position?"

Finding as much as you can about a candidate's history before the interview—the more the better—is important (though do make sure you stay on the right side of the law), but recruiters mustn't forget to discover and find new things during the interview. Elevate candidates' curiosity by finding out the reasons why they did what they did. You are particularly looking to identify intellectual curiosity and which candidates demonstrate these traits. You want to know not just how they talk about their curiosity and being curious, but if they demonstrate these behaviors. Some clues might be found in the following:

- *Pursuing challenges:* Does the candidate talk about situations in their work history when they discovered a solution to a problem no one else had thought about before?
- *Fixing what needs fixing:* Does the candidate describe when and how they creatively manage stressful or difficult situations? Intellectually curious people are natural problem solvers.
- *Thirst for knowledge:* Has the candidate researched the company? It's great to hear not only about the company itself, but also a few of its competitors and the industry as a whole.
- *Connecting the dots:* Does the candidate see how the organization fits in the market and ask questions that go beyond messages that can be collected in your marketing communications and collateral?
- *Heart:* Do you feel passion and energy when the candidate speaks of interests outside of work? Passion can move mountains. If you embrace your inner four-year-old, you'll recognize these better. Is the candidate asking "Why"? Do you recognize professional stories and future ambitions? As a recruiter, you have to value candidates who have a bigger picture and prioritize curiosity.

It's often the case that managers hire candidates who have long and quality industry experience, but it's also possible that these professionals are too stuck in their comfortable way of doing things and are likely to revert to a standard "playbook." The right candidates are those who are seeking knowledge and put effort into mastering new information quickly, regardless of their familiarity with the industry. Leaders are often dedicated to motivating their teams and ensuring that they're growing and developing. Intellectually curious people take care of this by themselves. Curious employees learn, improve, develop, and grow by finding and creating new informal and formal learning opportunities through conversations with other professionals and looking for new challenges. They're not waiting for their employers or managers to motivate them and create opportunities for them to learn and develop. Employees who have a strong drive for learning about people and their situations, problems, and successes are more likely to bring innovative new strategies and ideas to their organization. These are the people who never choose to sit back and wait for the next assignment. They proactively approach their manager or supervisor with new solutions for old and existing problems. They also have different ideas about how to stay ahead of competitors. If you're thinking about hiring people who come from outside your industry, decision-making confidence, professional presence, and inclusive leadership are likely just some of the benefits you'd experience. Remember, people who are willing to change industries are by default curious, brave, and not afraid of change.

Curiosity is rarely seen in the list of core competencies for recruiters. Yet it's widely noted as directly related to the success of those deemed as leaders in their field, and we can say that curiosity is an underlying competency that leads to more visible competencies. So while it is not listed, it is critically important for recruiters for several reasons:

- They'll know their business better, including understanding the organization and team goals, the challenges and risks, the actual work, and how any or all of these help the organization—its growth plans, its products, its market.
- They'll know teams better. They'll understand people, leadership styles, cultures, hiring capabilities, internal talent pools, and possible successors.
- They'll understand the target candidate profile better, and what capabilities are needed and why, plus the targets' backgrounds and sources of top talent for roles.
- They'll understand why diversity is important and what types of talent are underrepresented and needed to add to the team and why. They'll also know what kinds of challenges diverse hires would face and ways to set them up for inclusion—and thereby success.
- They'll understand internal and external metrics, the internal barriers to more speed, quality, and diversity, and how they can improve. They'll also bring external market insights, especially regarding compensation, that would help improve the ROI of recruiting efforts.

In general, by hiring intellectually curious recruiters, you'll get a more creative team: When traditional sourcing, assessment, and closing strategies and tactics aren't working or giving you the intended result, having creative people on the team is essential. Having intellectually curious people in recruitment helps deliver the talent the business will need to move forward and get to the next level. To do any of these things successfully, recruiters have to be curious and ask questions.

• • •

In the world of recruiters, curiosity is a key to success. Once you, as a recruiter, know the business leaders, what they're expecting from you, and how you can make things better and easier—this includes planning, being proactive, setting expectations, building, finding, inquiring, and leading—all of these things will ensure that you are successful for the future, not just for today.

For further reading, we recommend:
"The Business Case for Curiosity," by Francesca Gino (*Harvard Business Review*, September–October 2018)

LEADERS' WISDOM:
THE POWER OF CURIOSITY
• • •

We had a great example of curiosity being a huge value-add, as well as talking to the business in the right way, at a prior company I worked with. It involved a wind power farm in northern England where we needed to hire 400 wind power engineers in something ridiculous—like six months or so—to get the operation up and running. So the recruiting leader at the time took it upon herself and her team to not just start the recruitment process but meet with the business where it wanted to be met by going actually to the wind power plant, seeing where these blades were constructed and manufactured. These blades are almost the length of two football fields—enormous! The motors and the housing were as big as a two-story building. Just by going in there and being curious, asking questions about the supply chain, the manufacturing of these power plants and these windmills, plus the cadence of how they're built, how they're designed, how the wind farm is executed and rolled out, gave her tremendous insight into prioritizing the roles. It was great for partnering and being credible with the business and with facing off with the business, because suddenly she was speaking their language. When somebody talked about a part or about a certain process, she had been there, done that, and seen it happen on the plant floor. This then equipped her to be more credible, not just with the business leaders and the hiring managers but with the candidates, as she and her team in the UK were screening these wind power engineers and could tell which of the candidates were really on track. That helped accelerate the project tremendously and we got kudos not just from HR, but from the UK GM of the business too. I still have the document today which says, thanks to TA, they were able to get the project done ahead of time, under budget, and with the right talent in place to execute it.

—**Fernando Delgado, Global Head, Executive Talent Acquisition, Johnson & Johnson**

7.

EMPATHY AND LISTENING SKILLS
• • •

Empathy is about the ability to see the world through someone else's eyes. And, to quote Michael Ventura, author of *Applied Empathy*, "To connect with people, you have to understand them." This chapter will explore: What is empathy? Why is empathy important in recruiting? Why is listening important? What is empathetic listening, and how do we listen empathetically?

There are various definitions of empathy. Empathy can be the ability to understand and share the feelings of another. Others define it as the capacity to understand or feel what another person is experiencing from within their frame of reference; that is, the capacity to place yourself in another's position or put yourself in someone else's shoes. And there is a difference between cognitive empathy, affective or emotional empathy, and somatic empathy.

For our purposes we're going to focus on two types of empathy – affective and cognitive. Affective empathy, also called emotional empathy, is the capacity to respond with an appropriate amount of emotion to another's mental state. Our ability to empathize in this way is based on our being affected by another's emotional state. Affective empathy is further divided into two subcategories: Empathetic concern, which is compassion for others in response to their suffering; and personal distress—self-centered feelings or discomfort and anxiety in response to another's suffering. Cognitive empathy is the capacity to understand another's perspective and is further divided into three subcategories: (1) Perspective taking—the tendency to spontaneously adopt another psychological perspective; (2) fantasy—the tendency to identify with fictional characters; and (3) tactical or strategic empathy—the deliberate use of perspective taking to achieve a certain desired end. It's important to note that affective and cognitive empathy are independent from one another in that someone who strongly empathizes emotionally is not necessarily good at understanding another's perspective.

Why is empathy essential in recruiting? Empathy is a vital capability for both life and business, and it's also one of the key components of emotional intelligence. Emerging business strategies focus on emotionally competent leaders, and emotionally competent recruiters can identify emotionally competent leaders. We have therefore come to the conclusion that developing empathy is crucial for your survival as a recruiter, because understanding your candidates is critical if you really want to effectively align to leading roles in your organization.

Not that many people are natural-born empathetic leaders: It isn't easy for everyone to identify, process, and resonate with other people's emotions. But the good news is that empathy can be developed and practiced and sharpened as a skill through patience and exercise. You can't learn empathy, but you can practice being empathetic. In other words, technically, it's a skill that can be improved through practice and experience, but not one you can develop through textbooks.

As noted, to be empathetic, you need to develop the capacity to put yourself in someone else's shoes. A person's emotional reaction to events is a matter of perspective, and being empathetic toward others is vital to understanding their motives and circumstances. Perhaps not every action that a person takes looks like a well-intended one, but empathy requires that we start by believing the best of people. That doesn't mean you have to agree with everything, and being empathetic also does not create an obligation for you.

Empathy also requires vulnerability—that is, admitting that you don't know something in order to find out more about that person— especially if you are in front of someone you disagree with. Showing vulnerability can be a challenge because it isn't a trait commonly associated with recruiters. But you can't read anyone's mind (though recruiters are often expected to summarize a candidate's experience and motivations and predict their future outcome in an organization). So vulnerability takes courage. You and your team, the organization's leadership team, your client or clients, and your candidates are one system and you should support each other. It is important that you, as a recruiter, are brave and show your strength by asking candidates to help you more fully understand their purpose and passion, instead of hypothesizing it for them.

Listening, more than anything else, can significantly improve the quality of our empathetic interactions. Empathetic listening, also called "active listening" or "reflective listening," is the ability to listen with the sincere intention of understanding other people's values, opinions, and ideas. It is the practice of being attentive and responsive to others' input during conversations. As an empathetic listener, you invest an effort to understand other people's perspectives.

But it too has to be trained. Think about it. We expect other people to understand us, but we rarely put ourselves in their shoes. We want other people to resonate with our views, but we might not give them the chance to express their opinions. And even if they do, or offer some constructive criticism, we don't always return the favor. The result for some is that our day-to-day interactions could become a cold exchange with no real connection, no empathy between the people in that conversation. But if we're willing to listen instead of talk, to understand instead of criticize, and to comfort instead of judge, we can easily transform that conversation into an authentic human interaction.

In your role as a recruiter, candidly, after hours and hours of back-to-back calls or video interviews with candidates, active listening can get turned off. However, in this fast-paced world, one of the most challenging things you must do is exercise patience and listen to others before expressing your own opinions and plans. In other words, you need to return to being humans interacting with, and recruiting, humans. And as a reminder: When you talk, you repeat only what you already know, but when you listen, you have the opportunity to hear and learn something new. Since we as recruiters are oriented toward finding out new facts about our candidates, listening is the skill that best describes what we do.

THREE DIMENSIONS OF EMPATHETIC LISTENING

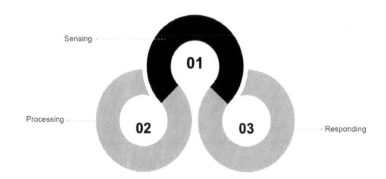

There are three dimensions of active empathetic listening: Sensing, processing, and responding. These three dimensions show us how well a person can feel emotions, process them, and come up with a response.

If you want to improve your qualities as an empathetic listener, you need to work on these things:

- *Presence:* You should be focused on what the other person is talking about, not just be present in physical terms. In order to be present, it is important to minimize external distractions and not to plan your own response while someone is talking. Carefully sit with that statement: Do not plan your own response when someone else is talking.

- *Compassion:* Compassion is the most important component of empathetic listening. It is the ability of the listener to identify with the other person's emotional experience. Even if you haven't experienced the same situation, you can try to find similarities in your experiences.

- *Wisdom:* If a person is sharing emotionally important content with you, it's very likely that the person trusts your judgment and experience. Wisdom includes the input of both understanding the speaker's input and examining the circumstances around the problem to better grasp all the factors involved.

- *Non-judgment:* Being nonjudgmental means holding back from criticizing another party, whether doing so out loud or in your thoughts. Even when you disagree with something the other person said, you need to consider they have their own reasons for acting the way they do.

- *Trustworthiness:* If the other person is speaking to you about emotional matters, it's crucial to keep what they say in confidence. However, if they ask that you support them by mediating a conflict with another party, and give you permission to share, you may discuss the details of the conversation.

- *Patience:* Even with close colleagues and friends, it can be challenging to disclose emotional experiences. It may take a speaker time to find the words that they want to say and feel comfortable enough to express them, so be patient and allow them the time they need.

- *Responsiveness:* Although empathetic listening means listening to the other party without interjecting your input, there will be likely a time when the speaker wants to hear what you think. In this case, it may help to clarify by asking, "Would you like to hear what I think about this?" "What kind of feedback would you like from me?"

Why is practicing empathetic listening important for your recruitment career? First, it creates better working relationships: People are more willing to share their experience with you if you can listen empathetically. This way, you're building trust and more positive interactions in the workplace from the very beginning. Second, the practice likely also leads to increased productivity. Teams always work better when coworkers trust and understand each other, and that leads to less conflict, greater output, and better problem solving. Workplace challenges frequently require teammates collaborating to find solutions. If you have a history of trust and open sharing with your coworkers, you may feel more comfortable proposing new approaches to workplace issues. Finally, when you develop the habit of considering others' feelings, you may be more likely to act kindly and compassionately in your day-to-day life—and the world can always use more people like you, in the workplace and out!

CREATING THE CONDITIONS FOR EMPATHETIC LISTENING

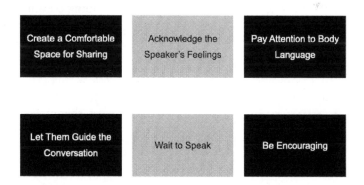

How to listen empathetically? First, create a comfortable space for sharing. If you provide a safe place for discussion, your candidate may be more likely to confide in you and in this way, you can also feel more comfortable. An interview can be stressful, but if the candidate sees you're calm, they'll respond by calming down and you're more likely to get a better read on their skills and competencies. It might be useful to practice deep breathing so that you'll be more present and attentive before the conversation starts. Acknowledge the speaker's feelings: When you listen to someone empathetically, it's good to let them know and be aware that you're considering their feelings. You can do this with short praises like, "Oh, I understand," or, "That must've been hard for you," or, "I see you weren't very happy about that." Pay attention to body language: Candidates' body posture or gestures can show they're not feeling comfortable. They might tap their feet, not sit up straight, or show that they're nervous in other ways. If this is the case, you should respond with more affirmations and also maintain a confident posture yourself, while speaking slowly and calmly. Let them talk and guide the conversation.

If there are breaks in the conversation, wait until the candidate speaks again. In fact, wait to speak in general: If you manage to reserve your opinion until the other person asks for it, you'll demonstrate that you value their input and respect their wishes. If you hear, "What do you think?" you may offer your opinion; but if not, it would be best to just listen and give small acknowledgments. Be encouraging. If someone is facing a situation or challenge that they don't know how to manage, it's more likely that they'll confide in you. If you're asked for input, your role can be to encourage them by saying something like, "I can see that you're able to manage this challenge." This way, the person you're talking to should feel more confident in the present and future situations.

The point of these interactions is to let the candidate speak to get to know everything about them that you're interested in. In order to make the right decisions about getting candidates into the process, you'll need a lot of information—and the more you get, the better your judgment will be.

Here are 10 strategies to develop empathetic listening:

1. It's not about you! Your conversation partner should be above your needs in every conversation.
2. Put your phone away.
3. Be an active listener. Empathetic listening and active listening are synonymous.
4. Refrain from criticism. Empathetic listening means a high degree of emotional intelligence. When someone shares something important or emotionally significant, refrain from evaluations, criticism, or negative feedback.
5. Adjust your body language. An open body language will allow

people to have a more relaxed posture and will make them feel safe and welcome to share.

6. Paraphrase. Paraphrasing is one of the most effective strategies for empathetic listening, because you're letting your conversation partner know that you understand their perspective. Paraphrasing, clarifying questioning, and remembering details are key for empathetic listening.

7. Ask open-ended questions.

8. Don't give unsolicited advice. Offering unsolicited advice is the worst thing you can do when you're looking to establish an emotional connection.

9. Don't fill up the silence. You may feel awkward during those moments of silence that are usual in any conversation (many people do), but silence—if you know how to use it—can be a powerful tool for establishing an authentic connection. Conversation is not a constant exchange of words. There are other ways, such as allowing the other person to gather their thoughts or simply using your body language, that help you express empathy and build an authentic connection. You can use silence to allow the other person to take charge or time to process your input and come up with an answer. Don't always fill up the space.

10. Relax. They are more likely to be relaxed if you are.

To develop and practice the skill of empathy, you should be mindful of all of these things in every conversation. When you're in a situation where someone is speaking to you in confidence, consider using these phrases to show them that you're listening empathetically: "I understand what you're saying"; "I identify with what you're going through"; "Thanks for sharing this with me." Empathetic listening is the foundation of effective communication and one of the secrets to lasting relationships. When you're ready to put aside your personal views and seek empathy with others, people will gravitate toward you. That, in turn, will result in authentic relationships and fruitful business partnerships.

We now suggest that you reread this entire chapter and consider the role of empathy in conversations with your client—specifically at the outset of a search. As discussed, communications with stakeholders are key to a search's success, and creating the conditions for empathetic listening during stakeholder interviews will further support your success delivering during the recruitment process.

For further reading, we recommend:

Applied Empathy: The New Language of Leadership, by Michael Ventura (Atria Books, 2018)

LEADERS' WISDOM:
COMPASSION AND KINDNESS GO A LONG WAY

● ● ●

When I think about things like authenticity, empathy, reliability, plus interest and passion—these are qualities that we look for in any executive coming to Providence. These attributes align with our mission of serving the poor and the vulnerable. It's the standard we would want and expect of our executives. We are blessed to work for an organization that has brilliant people, highly educated physicians, nurses, and business leaders with advanced degrees. The approach that generally doesn't work well is being the know-it-all and speaking just to be heard. What resonates with leaders? Well, when I look at high-performing leaders, regardless of how capable they are, critical factors to success are servant leadership and influence, which are built into all our job descriptions. Top-tier talent advisors understand the market internally and externally and know exactly what the business is looking for to be successful. They can tell the story of how a particular internal candidate may not necessarily be qualified on the surface but to bridge their skills gap getting the skills needed to be successful. That happens frequently.

Maybe just because I've been in the healthcare industry and nonprofit world for so long, but anytime that I've seen an executive recruiter or a leader showing up and not being authentic or genuine, I've not seen that approach to be successful. It's a road to nowhere because the recruiter is not communicating with that person if it's a candidate or hiring executive. It's like an ego match with one another. To build and cultivate a relationship— and I don't care if it's the most senior executive—I'm just going to be my authentic self. People appreciate that. I'm not the person with all the answers. I see better outcomes when leaders say, "I have something to add to this conversation that is substantively impactful as opposed to just wanting to say something to sound smart." That's not going to advance us forward… I believe people today need to check their egos at the door. It doesn't matter what job title we have.

Hope is missing in our world and society, and I think if you can bring compassion and kindness to any interaction, then that's a unique thing that unfortunately does not happen very often. People remember it. Even if you don't have all the capabilities needed such as strategic agility, consulting skills, or business acumen to be a successful executive talent advisor, I would hire someone with these qualities in a heartbeat, because we can train in the other areas. The heart, the willingness, the attitude, the passion, the kindness, the compassion—they all go a long way.

—Russell Podgorski, Executive Director, Executive Recruiting, Providence

8.

PURPOSE
• • •

merican humorist and novelist Mark Twain was famously quoted as saying, "The two most important days in your life are the day you're born, and the day you find out why." Organizations today have to critically review whether their product or service enhances and improves the lives of those it touches, as well as consider other externalities such as the impact on the environment and the social impact of their business. This starts with senior leaders being engaged around the "why": Why do we exist, and why do we seek to deliver beyond just competing consumer demands and profits? How does an organization's recruiting strategy adjust to support purpose? There is a significantly missed opportunity to measure conviction and passion for an organization's purpose in the hiring process. Many executives will be naturally curious and look to connect the company's purpose to their own.

This chapter will explore organizational purpose: What is it? What's its benefit? How do you articulate purpose to candidates? How do you create alignment in the recruiting process and define culture, purpose, and engagement? How do you help clients and candidates find each other with purpose in mind?

First, however, we should define "purpose." Unlike a typical mission statement, a company's purpose aims primarily to address the reason the business does what it does. While it outlines the overall direction of the business, it may also incorporate specific aspects like key focus areas, strategic partnerships, and target audiences. Another definition that explains the difference between mission, vision, and purpose might be that a good mission statement and vision statement are best suited for internal organizational guidance. Purpose, however, keeps you focused on why you exist. Vision aligns you with your goal, and mission empowers you on how you will accomplish it. When a supporter connects with your purpose, they will believe in your mission. Organizational purpose is meaningful and an enduring reason to exist, and answers the "why." Why are we here? Why are we doing business? It's the organization's fundamental reason for being. Organizational purpose aligns with long-term financial performance, provides a clear context for daily decision-making, and unifies and motivates relevant stakeholders. If the organization wants to achieve sustainable growth, the most important thing to be done is to align to purpose. If employees are working with good intentions, but are not aligned with the company's purpose, their productivity may be in opposition to the goals that are required for long-term success.

To make a whole company purpose-driven, you need to start from the top. Connecting leaders with purpose will make employees connect with it too. It is only leaders and employees who are connected to a company's purpose who can drive it toward its goal. The adoption of a company's purpose by its employees will lead to innovation, cooperation, and organizational success. Organizations with a strong sense of purpose talk about it all the time and everywhere. They post it on their websites and printed materials, display it on the office walls, and speak about it in advertisements and at all levels of the organization. Poor leadership is the number one reason for poor engagement, and research tells us that only about 70% of the workforce is engaged in their work. Therefore, having leaders connected to the company's purpose will create a workforce engaged in their work and connected to the company's purpose too.

Purpose is not ideology. As we stated earlier, it is a bottom-line-focused strategy and provides competitive advantage. What matters most to employees today is meaningful work, not just a paycheck. As an example, if a construction worker is asked to remove a children's playground, it is likely it is not only about what their income is for getting it done. At the end of the day, they'd probably like to know why. Are they going to build a better one, or a prettier one, afterward? Or is it just to make space for a new gas station? It makes a difference to know. If recruiters are able to articulate organizational purpose to future candidates, they're going to be able to recruit leaders who are motivated by the same goals and likely to make a contribution to the organization much more quickly.

Finding candidates who are inspired by the purpose of the

organization and motivated by the same purpose will help you build teams that believe in your company's purpose too. To accentuate this point, in our own experience in making offers to many very senior executive candidates, we would cover in our discussion all the usual compensation and benefits items that were part of the offer as normal and relatively quickly. However, the page in the discussion document that the candidates most seemed to linger on and want to talk more about was the one that outlined the impact they were going to make on the product, the business, the industry – out of all the parts of the offer, they were most interested in the "why." If you ever wondered why a candidate would take a role for less compensation then they are currently earning, you now know: Purpose.

As a recruiter, your role is to articulate organizational purpose to candidates. It's not something that can be imposed on employees. The hiring process is an opportunity for both sides to find a natural alignment between individual and organizational purpose. This is also a significant opportunity for recruiters to measure candidates' conviction and passion at the outset. Prioritizing concise and clear communication during the hiring process is one of the most vital strategies that every recruiter needs to practice. Make sure there is no room for misinterpretation. A well-articulated organizational purpose is always easy to understand. What strengthens its value is providing examples of how it is seen in the organization.

HOW DO YOU ALIGN PURPOSE IN THE RECRUITMENT PROCESS?

First, be sure that you as a recruiter can clearly articulate the organization's purpose and be transparent with it in every candidate conversation. Second, create or encourage the creation of specific and concise role descriptions and make sure you ask the client the right questions at the very beginning of the search. Too many role descriptions are not clear and don't have the company's purpose written into them. Worse, if a posting is drafted from such a description, it might very well attract people with varying goals, many of which will not align, thereby wasting valuable recruiting time. Third, ask the right questions of your prospects and candidates to find out whether your candidates are connected to purpose. Here are some suggestions:

"What was the purpose of the company you last worked for?"

"Did that specific company's purpose inspire you? Why or why not?"

"What would be one that could inspire you?"

Finally, spend time with candidates in many ways, and with every one of them. More interactions with candidates will help you to identify their purpose and values.

The days when a leadership recruiting process was dedicated to finding the best résumé among many are gone. Today, this process is focused on finding exceptional leaders, which for the company means not only alignment on performance but on purpose. Hiring for alignment is not the same as hiring for "culture fit." Culture is basically "how" an organization operates. The term has been embedded in recruiting for years and is established as the foundation of many corporate recruiting processes. However, it's now taken on more of a tribal meaning; that is, people who "look like us, think like us, work like us, live like us." A hiring process built around an undefined notion of culture fit is fraught with bias. In some organizations, it has become a weaponized phrase that interviewers use as a blanket term to reject candidates. Reframe "culture fit" to be "culture-add" (people who align with the "why" of the company or its purpose), and seek out candidates who add to the culture instead of fitting into it. This provides organizations with a richer and diverse culture.

Here are the benefits of aligning purpose early in the process, according to Neelie Verlinden of AIHR:

Reduced turnover: If you hire someone who fits your purpose and your overall organization's values, they will be much more inclined to stay with the company for a long time. This means that for an extraordinary recruitment result, recruiters should focus on both role fit and purpose fit. Recognizing both but setting purpose fit as a priority during your recruitment process will help you set the foundation for a lower turnover rate.

Increased quality of hire: Employees who feel at home in the organization they work for are genuinely happier and have a positive impact on their productivity and their engagement. They'll need less time to become fully operational, and they'll boost their colleagues' morale while they're at it.

Increased employee engagement: There's no secret recipe for employee engagement, but if there was, one of the ingredients would be purpose. People who work for a company that shares their values and whose purpose they're inspired by will do so much more wholeheartedly than those who don't recognize themselves in the organization.

Increased productivity: All of these elements lead to increased employee productivity.

Better referrals: Employee referrals have always been a great way of recruiting new people. Referrals tend to be operationally faster, more productive, and more engaged and stay with the company longer. You should manage this carefully, and it must be done properly, otherwise it can be a mechanism for inadvertently reducing the proportion of underrepresented groups in the organization.

Measuring conviction and passion for the organization's purpose in the hiring process will allow naturally curious candidates to connect the company's purpose to their own. It will also empower candidates at the outset by establishing a more sophisticated talent acquisition process that supports the business as it grows. If recruiters manage to nurture organizational purpose in hired candidates from the start of the process, it will ensure that purpose will be present and alive in the organization.

If an organization stands only for profit, power, or bureaucracy, there's a very good chance employees fall into the "job" mindset and work for a paycheck. Management expert Peter Drucker once said, "To make a living is no longer enough, work also has to make a life." It is this purpose at work that people are looking for. We recommend you include an authentic purpose message in every recruiting conversation. Look for connections in a candidate's purpose to the organization's, as you're the one connecting the dots. Individual, team, and organizational purpose might sound like purpose overload, but in fact, it's just a process of building a single story line that helps candidates see how they fit into the bigger picture.

For further reading, we recommend:

"Purpose-Driven Companies Evolve Faster Than Others," by Caterina Bulgarella (*Forbes*, September 21, 2018)

"Your Company's Purpose Is Not Its Vision, Mission or Values," by Graham Kenny (*Harvard Business Review*, September 2014)

LEADERS' WISDOM:
SAYING "NO" AND USING DATA AS LEVERAGE

• • •

There was one situation where there was not great communication amongst the hiring leaders of two parts of the business, which were both involved in us hiring eight leaders against essentially one profile, with some nuances between the roles. The issue became that these different group leaders didn't really think through what the must-haves were and what these new hires would be doing. Also, there were some strategic questions that came up as we started to comb the market around the job, for instance, "Who leads the marketing piece?" or "Where does this other role sit on the asset team?" Basically, there were fundamental questions that were coming up that were precluding us from moving forward with candidates and getting them over the line. So, Pinar put a plan together to get everybody together in a room, get them all on the same page, and let them know what we heard from the market. She pushed them on the key questions and kept driving the issues, even though a lot of people wanted to punt it. In this instance, when we were trying to attract the high-caliber candidate that the CEO was really keen on, we needed to get these questions answered in order to get the talent interested. So, we had to sit down and consult and get two Executive Vice Presidents together, and then get the CEO involved, asking for his feedback and what he envisioned for this model. This was a prime example of when we had to consult and go back and say no to the senior leaders, use leverage, and move the business forward in a different way. We were "pleasant with an edge": We helped them understand by laying out the facts from what we were hearing in the market, plus from our benchmarking with our internal talent. We basically used the data to help our argument and to help them think about the bigger picture, which was as much about change management as anything else.

—Lisa DiPaolo, SVP Human Resources, and Pinar Hanna, Head of Global Executive Search, Ipsen

9.

EMOTIONAL INTELLIGENCE
• • •

Understanding and managing your own and others' emotions will make you a stronger leader. According to Steve Gutzler, a renowned thought leader and speaker on leadership, emotional intelligence, and personal transformation, "Emotional intelligence can be the game changer to higher performance and personal leadership." This chapter will explore what emotional intelligence is, why it's important, the value of emotional intelligence, its importance for recruiters, and the indicators of emotional intelligence.

WHAT IS EMOTIONAL INTELLIGENCE?

In the *Dictionary of Psychology*, Andrew Coleman defines emotional intelligence this way: "Emotional intelligence is the capacity to be aware of, control, and express one's emotions and to handle interpersonal relationships, judiciously and empathetically. Emotional intelligence stands for proceeding, using, understanding, and managing emotions." Some studies have shown that individuals with high emotional intelligence have better mental health, better job performance, and better leadership skills. Research says that 67% of all abilities that are important and necessary for great leaders' performance are connected to this trait, and it is twice as important as general intelligence or any technical expertise because emotions are a part of every human interaction. Not so long ago, people were advised to leave their emotions at home when heading to work or exclude emotions in the process of making decisions. This point of view aligned to the attitude that decisions should be based solely on rationality and facts. However, this perspective is changing. Developed emotional intelligence helps people better understand feedback, understand themselves, and understand others. People with high emotional intelligence better manage their strengths as well as their weaknesses, producing greater outcomes.

Emotionally intelligent people are generally more balanced and are able to approach problems calmly. In a 2017 session held during the Recruiting Trends and Talent Tech Conference, Caroline Stokes predicted that in the future, emotional intelligence would be a top skill for employees. She cited the US Air Force, which had recently switched to more emotionally intelligent recruiters and saved $3 million in operating costs.

Similarly, the World Economic Forum tells us that developing emotional intelligence skills is something that all companies should focus on because "emotional intelligence sets star performers apart from the rest of the pack."

And the research doesn't stop there. Multiple studies have found over the past few decades that those managers and employees with higher emotional intelligence are relatively more productive and have better promotion records and retention rates. Organizations that either assess for, or train in, emotional intelligence factors are also likely to be more successful compared with those that do not.

Emotional intelligence is important for recruiters for two reasons: First, because you develop relationships that are based on trust and communication, emotional intelligence is an integral part of everything you do. Consider presenting new opportunities to candidates, finding out and understanding their motivations, listening to their concerns. Second, when you are able to develop emotional intelligence and recognize it in candidates, you add value to the organization beyond your contribution.

Let's now consider the fundamental skills of a recruiter and put "emotionally intelligent" at the top. As an emotionally intelligent recruiter, you're able to develop relationships based on trust and communication. You can identify emotional intelligence in other leaders, and new recruiting approaches will imply that developed emotional intelligence is required.

Now let's consider emotional intelligence applied in a new recruiting approach. Traditional recruiting approaches are often cost-driven; they drive diversity through sourcing. In traditional approaches, recruiters are expected to understand job preferences, are order takers and matchmakers, and have the ability to broker connections. But let's apply emotional intelligence to our recruiting approach. What happens? A new approach would then look like this: It would be quality driven, and recruiters would have the ability to understand a candidate's career motivation, be executive career coaches, be able to consult on role design based on industry knowledge, and drive diversity through the definition of needs.

INDICATORS OF EMOTIONAL INTELLIGENCE

Psychologist and author Daniel Goleman posits five characteristics of emotional intelligence.

01 Self-awareness

02 Self-regulation

03 Motivation

04 Empathy

05 Social skills

Most senior recruiters identify with these five traits to a certain level, but only those who are willing, ready, and motivated to reach complete mastery will actually realize their full potential. Improving these qualities will require constant attention.

Self-awareness: Being self-aware means that you'll be able to recognize your own strengths and weaknesses and know and recognize the circumstances under which they work best. Recruiters who are self-aware, besides recognizing their own mood and emotions, are also aware of how they affect and influence other people.

Self-regulation: Self-regulation, or self-management, is a critical factor in successful collaboration in the workplace. When you regulate yourself, you actually control and redirect your impulses. To practice self-regulation, focus on self-awareness first, then recognize how to control your reactions and recognize how much to take on, before stress and emotions start to get in the way.

Motivation: It's great for recruiters to be self-driven, self-motivated, and highly organized. Recruiters who are motivated tend to take control of their schedule and maximize their efficiency to increase output. An important part of motivation in the recruiting industry is continually leveraging it, especially after failure.

Empathy: There is no successful senior recruiter without developed empathy. As noted in the previous chapter, empathy is the ability to understand other people's emotions—those that are exposed and especially those that are wrapped up. It's about bringing a personal level of understanding to a relationship.

People or social skills: Being a "people person" is more than having the ability to listen and act. It's about building trust through ongoing communication and finding common ground with other people in order to build rapport. The best leadership recruiters build rapport at a very early stage in their exchanges with both clients and prospects or candidates. In fact, in some cases, it might be the most important thing they do as much of what happens afterward depends on that "first trust" being built early on.

Great news—emotional intelligence is a skill that can be practiced and developed! It's not something we're born with. We recommend practicing observing how you feel—try to notice and recognize where that specific emotion is showing up as a physical feeling in your body and what that sensation feels like. Pay attention to how you behave. Observe how you feel when you're experiencing a specific emotion and try to recognize how that affects your day-to-day life. It will be easier for you to manage your emotions if you're aware of how you react to them. Take responsibility for your feelings—you produce your emotions and behaviors; these don't come from anyone else. As American First Lady Eleanor Roosevelt famously said, "No one can make you feel inferior without your consent."

When you accept responsibility for how you feel and behave, all areas of your life will be positively affected. Take the time to celebrate the positive, but don't ignore the negative. Positive emotions will make you feel more resilient and more likely to develop fulfilling relationships, so take time to celebrate them. However, reflecting on negative feelings is just as important. Understanding why you have negative feelings will help you become a more fully rounded individual and more able to deal with negative issues in the future. When you've developed emotional intelligence, you will be quality driven and have a greater understanding of candidates' motivations. You will be less of a broker and more of an executive career coach, contribute more meaningfully on role design, and drive diversity through the definition of needs.

For further reading, we recommend:
Primal Leadership: Realizing the Power of Emotional Intelligence, by Daniel Goleman, Annie McKee, and Richard Boyatzis (Harvard Business School Press, 2002)

LEADERS' WISDOM:
SOMETIMES YOU JUST HAVE TO PICK THE BEST-LOOKING ORANGE

• • •

When you're dealing with businesspeople, you have to speak business, and that's not just about PowerPoint presentations but due diligence too. It's showing them data around what our funnel metrics look like. What are we starting off with? How many people did we source? Who responded to us and who did we cut? Who made it from the qualified list we presented to who was interviewed? It's also about showing the due diligence around, and owning the credibility of, the fact that we know all the market players. We've done a methodical job of sourcing and researching all of our top 40 competitors. And then we've also looked at adjacent industries where we may find this talent. It's really important to have structure around your research methodology that supports and helps build that trust. Show that you've thought ahead, are not just bringing candidates that are interested or raising their hand, but that you're conducting a due diligence effort so that when it comes to the end of your search, you feel good that you've turned over all the stones.

Saying that, the opposite could be true, and it's important to know what works in some situations. I love to use the analogy for those times when you have a really good candidate, but the hiring leader wants to keep looking. It's like when I go to the grocery store and I pick the best-looking orange off the top; I don't go to the bottom of the orange barrel every time to make sure that was the best one. Now, we're not dealing with oranges, but with massive amounts of compensation and somebody who can add a lot of value to your organization. However, there's the idea that sometimes we may keep looking for the sake of "keep looking" and that's not always the right solution either. I do think it does make a big difference in terms of trust that they are not going to have doubts about the hire, even if there are gaps, or this person wasn't exactly what they had in mind when they started the search, but there's a balance that has to be made at the end of the day as we don't want to lose great talent for the sake of overdone due diligence.

—**Dustin Fillion, Director, Talent Acquisition, Discover Financial Services**

10

THE TRUSTED ADVISOR
• • •

Trust creates a strong foundation in all relationships, whether business or personal. Transactions can't take place without trust. Thousands of little deeds, words, ideas, and intentions combine to create it. Gaining trust doesn't happen overnight, and it requires time and effort. Trust is an attitude we exhibit toward people we think we can rely on; if they do indeed live up to our belief, they are trustworthy—and this means that trustworthiness is a characteristic, not an attitude. Trust and trustworthiness are therefore different concepts, yet in an ideal setting, people we trust are also trustworthy, and those who are trustworthy will also be trusted.

WHY IS TRUST IMPORTANT IN THE EXECUTIVE RECRUITMENT PROCESS?

During the executive search process, there are thousands of little moments and sources of information passed between a client and a candidate throughout the journey. In a relationship lacking trust, these interactions are chaotic and unstable. Being a trusted advisor means that you have the experience, training, knowledge, and subject-matter expertise to be trusted to advise your clients well, and they in turn have confidence in your opinion and direction throughout the process. The executive search process doesn't happen to you—recruiters are the conduit through which candidates and clients come closer together. But neither side will take that step without trust in your role to execute it successfully. Consider every small action over time during the search process as an opportunity to build trust.

This chapter will explore how the role of the trusted advisor evolves, the five stages of trust development, the four conditions of trust, recruiters as trusted advisors, and the top behaviors that enable trust. When someone calls you a "trusted advisor," it means that you have the business acumen, experience, training, knowledge, and subject-matter expertise that inspires confidence in you. The key word here isn't "advisor," but "trusted."

WHAT IS TRUST?

What does it mean to be trusted? "Trust" as a verb means to believe—if you believe in something or someone, then you trust them. To gain our clients' and candidates' trust, we must be believable—they must be sure that we will keep our word, do our part, and follow through on expectations set. Trust is not a technique or tool. We are trusted because of who we are, our way of being, not because of our polished exterior or expertly crafted communications.

FOUR CONDITIONS OF TRUST

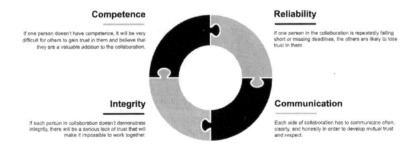

Competence

If one person doesn't have competence, it will be very difficult for others to gain trust in them and believe that they are a valuable addition to the collaboration.

Reliability

If one person in the collaboration is repeatedly falling short or missing deadlines, the others are likely to lose trust in them.

Integrity

If each person in collaboration doesn't demonstrate integrity, there will be a serious lack of trust that will make it impossible to work together.

Communication

Each side of collaboration has to communicate often, clearly, and honestly in order to develop mutual trust and respect.

As part of your evolution to trusted advisor, we assume that you've met the "needs satisfaction" requirement, and you're looking to move to the next level, which occurs on a personal level between you and another human being. It exists when you can affirmatively answer the following: "Are you trustworthy, dependable, respectful, fair?" These things are fundamental to any relationship, but they transcend the essentially transactional nature of most professional relationships.

When considering a collaborative, trusting relationship, according to Alyssa Gregory in her piece titled "4 Elements of Trust Needed in Successful Collaboration," you'll need to develop the following:

Competence: A collaborative relationship is going to fail if there is a gross mismatch of skills and experience between the people engaged. All sides of the collaboration need to have areas in which they excel, and a general understanding of the rest. If one person lacks a certain level of competence, it would be very difficult for others to gain trust in them to do and believe that they are a valuable addition to the collaboration.

Reliability: Reliability is important in all relationships, but it plays an even bigger role in collaborative relationships. If one person is repeatedly falling short or missing deadlines, the others are likely to lose trust in that person. Without having confidence that everyone is carrying their own weight, it can be a challenge to maintain collaboration.

Integrity: No one would ever enter collaboration if there was a risk that someone is going to gather up all the work and present it as their own. If each person in the collaboration doesn't demonstrate integrity, there'll be a serious lack of trust that will make it impossible to work together in the future.

Communication: Without communication, none of the other elements of trust matters. Each member in the collaboration has to communicate often, clearly, and honestly in order to develop mutual trust and respect. Collaboration is based on a meeting of minds and can't exist without it. In a collaboration where all parties give equally and share in the victories, they must clearly understand and be honest with each other for the partnership to succeed.

FIVE STEPS TO DEVELOPING TRUST

Once the conditions of trust are met, follow these five steps to developing trust as outlined by David Maister, Charles Green, and Robert Galford in *The Trusted Advisor*:

Engage: To build trust, you've got to get off on the right foot. To do so, you have to engage with the other person in a meaningful way. You have to be interested in them—or at least interested in the things you're discussing with them.

Listen: It is said that we have two ears and one mouth so we can listen twice as much as we speak. As we've detailed in the "Empathy and Listening Skills" chapter, active listening is one of the hardest and yet most important skills you can develop in your everyday life. In building trust, there is possibly no more important staff than good listening. Through good listening, you're able to remove your assumptions and judgments from the equation and get down to the underlying meaning behind what the other person is actually saying. So often, we waste our time when listening, just waiting for our turn to speak. Early in the conversation, we might quickly conclude that we understand the other person's point and thus we divert the majority of our attention to what we'll say next and leave only a sliver of remaining focus to the person speaking. This is a fundamental mistake we all make, but if you want to earn trust, it's vital that the other person feels as though they're being heard and understood.

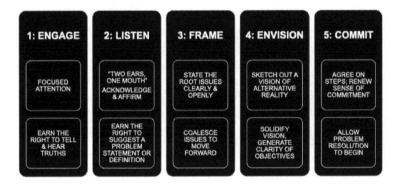

Frame: Showing you've understood the other person's perspective can be achieved in a number of ways, but the one we'll focus on here is called "framing." Framing is very similar to reflective listening in that you repeat what the other person has said or is trying to say so that they can either acknowledge as correct or fix your understanding. We touched on these earlier on consultative questioning. Try these short phrases: "So if I'm hearing you correctly, you're saying..."; or, "If I'm understanding you clearly, you're saying..." The power of framing in this way is that it invites the other person to clarify where they need to, while demonstrating your desire to actually understand them. You'll be surprised to discover through asking these questions just how often the other person will say. "Actually, what I meant to say was..." This is normal. Clear communication is an iterative skill that requires persistent practice. Don't take it personally if they correct you; in fact, it's a vital part of the process and should be looked at as a gift. Remember that, in a recruiter's world, we are helping our client solve a business problem through talent. Thus, if we frame the situation in that way, not only are we talking their language, but we are also driving the conversation to the next stage: Collective envisioning.

Envision: Once you've reached the point of understanding the other person and their wants and needs, you can move into the envisioning step. Here's where you collate everything you've dug up in the previous step to create a vision of the solution. By reflecting back what you hear that person saying, understanding the emotions underlying their words, and offering a solution that is sensitive to their needs, you're building a solid foundation of trust. Through this mechanism, the other person feels that this relationship is collaborative rather than combative. As a recruiter, you should also position the client as part of the solution so that the path forward, to which they will later commit, will include their active involvement.

Commit: This is ultimately where the rubber meets the road. Everything up to this point has just been words – now it's time for action. In the commitment phase, you're trying to clearly articulate the responsibilities each person will be accountable for, while spelling out any potential obstacles the chosen path might encompass. This might not seem like an important step, but skipping it would be a mistake. This is where you brainstorm and commit to a solution you can both abide by. Again, this is the stage where individual responsibilities are outlined, and timelines, expectations, and goals are agreed to.

By consistently implementing these five steps—engage, listen, frame, envision, commit—you'll start building a type of trust, in both your personal and professional life, you never thought possible.

THE EVOLUTION OF RECRUITER TO TRUSTED ADVISOR

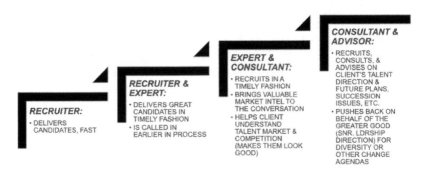

RECRUITER:
- DELIVERS CANDIDATES, FAST

RECRUITER & EXPERT:
- DELIVERS GREAT CANDIDATES IN TIMELY FASHION
- IS CALLED IN EARLIER IN PROCESS

EXPERT & CONSULTANT:
- RECRUITS IN A TIMELY FASHION
- BRINGS VALUABLE MARKET INTEL TO THE CONVERSATION
- HELPS CLIENT UNDERSTAND TALENT MARKET & COMPETITION (MAKES THEM LOOK GOOD)

CONSULTANT & ADVISOR:
- RECRUITS, CONSULTS, & ADVISES ON CLIENT'S TALENT DIRECTION & FUTURE PLANS, SUCCESSION ISSUES, ETC.
- PUSHES BACK ON BEHALF OF THE GREATER GOOD (SNR. LDRSHIP DIRECTION) FOR DIVERSITY OR OTHER CHANGE AGENDAS

Using the framework from Maister, Green, and Galford, let's look at the evolution of recruiter to trusted advisor. You likely see yourself somewhere in the first three levels—recruiter, recruiter and expert, or expert and consultant. Moving into the consultant and advisor level will put you in a new category of partnership. Clients will seek your advice on talent direction and future plans. At the same time, as your role evolves, you'll find yourself pushing back on behalf of the greater good, seeking to support larger change agendas in areas such as diversity or other processes. You'll elevate the business by being well connected in the industry, and you may see industry opportunities outside of your immediate remit—like the ability to attract a team of people instead of make just one hire—and present this opportunity to the client proactively. In a similar vein, just by the nature of your work, you collect significant industry intelligence, and the "consultant and advisor" level is the one where you share that data in a digestible way, potentially impacting the business at a broader level.

The trusted advisor is in the game for a long-term relationship, not short-term gain. If you want to develop long-term relationships and partnerships as a trusted advisor, you should be prepared to invest some time in meeting, calling, and generally staying in touch with people, especially when you don't have any work on the go or open positions for a client. Trusted advisors put clients first—the clients' interests in front of their own. If an advisor appears to be more interested in themselves than in trying to be of service to the client, distrust will come as a result. By being interested in other people, you can make more clients regard you as a trusted advisor in two months than you can in two years by trying to get others interested in you.

Trusted advisors are genuinely interested in their clients personally, and in their businesses. To become a trusted advisor, you need to work really hard to understand the client's underlying interests, not just surface wants. Seek to understand, and then to be understood. It is vital for you to take the time to dig below the surface and try to really understand why clients are asking you to do the work in a certain way. What's motivating them to do that? What underlying interests are causing them to take up certain positions on certain matters? Trusted advisors are reliable and they do what they say they'll do. So, make sure you deliver—and ideally overdeliver—on promises, even the small ones.

Referring back to earlier chapters, it is very important here to practice the "why," not just the "what." Dig deeper and understand the business more, and distinguish yourself by learning about the executive leader's or client's corner of the world. Be prepared and informed for the conversation with every executive you meet with. Differentiate yourself from others through assessing needs in detail. Meet with clients on a regular basis in order to strengthen your understanding of the group's goals, issues, current team talents, and hiring misfires and causes, even if you don't have open roles. Perhaps bring along some recent data you've picked up in other candidate conversations. Some corporate recruiting organizations have developed regular talent news updates that they share with senior business leaders to update them on the talent market, and these are often readily welcomed by executives.

As a recruiter, it's your role to refocus yourself and establish, or return to, a relationship with the function you support in a consultative, value-added way. This starts with the relationship between you and the hiring team. Cement your partnership role through quality focus—have an intimate knowledge of talent together with the right strategy to attract and engage. This is a set of skills as valuable as any other in any organization. As a coach and counsel to executive leaders, use data, anecdotal input, and strong business cases for change. You help strengthen your role as a trusted and valued partner to them by delivering in this way. Assume your role as business partner—take your seat at the table instead of waiting for an invitation. As a recruiter, you have a unique and strategic set of information, such as best brand communication practices, how to engage passive candidates, and so on. Similarly, by coaching leaders to view the recruitment process through the candidate's point of view, you'll shatter hiring practice paradigms and you'll have the clients' trust to tailor their recruiting approach accordingly.

Another point: Give your opinion when it's not requested. If you want to have an effective partnering relationship with a client, never ask permission to weigh in. If you are about to recommend four candidates to a senior leader, then list them in your preferred order. You have an opinion and you know the candidates intimately, so share your perspective. If you're participating in a debrief meeting after a panel interview, speak first. Don't wait for the client or another senior executive to weigh in and let it alter your opinion or worse, everyone else's. Be bold—be a strategic business partner, not a subordinate. Partnering isn't acquiescing; it's about having an equal share in the outcome. By educating yourself about the goals of the client and the business, and activating a series of initiatives that build knowledge, trust, and momentum, you as a recruiter and consultant can cultivate a true trusted advisor partnering relationship.

LEADERS' WISDOM:
IT TAKES TIME AND WORK TO BUILD TRUST AND RELATIONSHIPS

● ● ●

Trusted advisorship is all earned on the battlefield. Even with our most seasoned consultants that excel in this arena, there's occasionally a time when I introduce them to a new client and it takes a bit of work to get to that point of trust and partnership. It helps that the consultant is always in the market on that client's behalf and able to articulate the value proposition smartly, but where the rubber really meets the road is introducing great talent to our clients. The client feels you understand what they're going after. From that point, once you've earned their trust, then there's a very quick element of true camaraderie that emerges. Then that starts to bleed into late-night phone calls, texting, and so on. Relationships are created, and informal discussions go beyond the regular information shared.

I remember one client wanted to bring in an external search partner as there was a lack of trust on our capability versus a big search firm, but they really came back to us after we hit the ball out of the park with successfully landing those needs. Breaking that down to the actual search process: We hit the ground learning, understanding the business; then from there we netted a few hires. We really expanded our aperture to make sure that we were bringing forth the best diverse talent. Then, slowly over time, you start getting more and more requisitions and more and more hires. Now, you're in the market proactively and you've built mastery over the market and you're talking shop with the business leaders. Then you're able to push back, to provide some market feedback, and to correct the expectations that may be out of line. I think a business leader really values you as that trusted relationship develops. It's up to us to really articulate what the market will bear, basic market availability, plus a lens on what our competitors are doing, what compensation levels will actually work.

Once you get to a true trusted advisorship level, the game changes: Recently we've been working with our internal succession and development teams a lot within a specific business unit, as well as with the head of that unit, who directly reports to the CEO. We've been having discovery sessions as a platform to have these very exploratory, "fantasy-like" discussions with the business leaders about what they want, what the business needs to grow in the future. These are very freewheeling, open-ended discussions, which ended up in actual approved head count for us to launch a search around this wish list. It's a way of staying ahead of the business demand and really leveraging the leaders to help and to "work without a net," if you will.

—Aaron Kliner, Director, Executive Search and Integration, IBM

11.

TOP 10 BEHAVIORS OF A TRUSTED ADVISOR
• • •

U p to this point, we have discussed the competencies that drive successful leadership recruiting. But what does it look like in terms of day-to-day behavior with our clients? If you are able to capitalize on the theory and experiences above, then you'll be well on the way to being the advisor that we all seek to be, and you'll likely be exhibiting the following 10 behaviors:

1. Be committed: Build long-term relationships for long-term mutual gains, not short-term quick wins.

The trusted advisor is in the game for a long-term relationship, not short-term gain. If you want to develop long-term relationships and partnerships as a trusted advisor, you should be prepared to invest thoughtful time in meetings, calls, and generally staying in touch with people, especially when you don't have any work on the go or open positions for a client. It's incredibly important to understand the business and the business strategy far ahead of trying to understand an individual role or position.

In a similar vein, though the idea of leadership assimilation and post-hire onboarding is not always given the attention it deserves, it does not just have to be about "How is the new hire doing?" It's also good practice to keep in touch with your candidates after they have started. Not only can you learn and grow by asking them how they felt they were treated throughout the process, thereby improving your own performance, but at this level they are also likely to be important influencers in your client's business. Furthermore, they are probably also going to be clients at some point too.

It is also important to highlight that you must truly earn the "trust" in "trusted advisor." You have to rebuild and reinforce trust every time you sit down or interact with your client to provide extra value to your client. It's an issue of how professional you are, that you maintain complete confidentiality and utilize information only for your client's advantage. In the long run, you may be able to influence the client's strategic direction and assist them in improving in the broadest sense, ultimately assisting them in shaping a solution to their business challenges.

2. Be selfless: Put others' interests before your own.

Demonstrating that your prospects' and clients' needs come first is the most important thing you can do to build strong client relationships. You must be able to view their problems through their eyes and be able to properly express solutions to them, even if the solution comes from someone other than yourself. Being sincere in what you recommend and provide will go a long way toward gaining the client's trust and building a positive working relationship.

If an advisor appears to be more interested in themselves instead of trying to be of service to the client, distrust will result. You can get more clients who regard you as a trusted advisor in two months by being interested in others than you can in two years by trying to get others interested in you and what you do. As the well-known phrase goes: "To be interesting, be interested." Your investment of your time to listen to, to learn from, to read about a client to ensure that their interest and their success is ahead of your own success will continue to elevate your trusted advisor status within your client's eyes.

Ask about your client's goals. Investigate their thoughts. Using various approaches to collect data can offer you crucial information about what people expect from you and how you can meet those expectations.

Remember to follow through on your commitments as well. You must be able to meet a certain degree of expectation if you establish one. It's evident that you don't respect your client's priorities if you breach any promises you've made. Allow clients to quickly provide feedback and contact you via a variety of channels, such as phone, text, or email. You might also inform your clients about the times when you are most likely to be available and reply. They will come to perceive you as a trustworthy counsel as you exhibit your availability on a regular basis.

Trusted advisors also stay abreast of institutional challenges, news and press releases, and financial outcomes and are connected to market dynamics and trends overall. This allows the trusted advisor to make connections between business strategy and talent strategy before being asked about it. Thoughtful and prompt responses make clients feel as though you are on their side, looking out for them, and can be trusted to raise any issues that may affect them before they know it.

LEADERS' WISDOM:
BE GENUINELY INTERESTED IN THE OTHER PERSON
● ● ●

I ask my team to tell me a bit about their hiring managers or about a candidate that they recently spoke to. The bit I want to know is not that they're this SVP of Engineering, or whatever, but that they collect cars and do rallying at weekends, or they recently bought their partner a horse, or something. That's what I want to know—I want to get into the internal, not just the external, profile. Obviously, you have to do it with humility, and you have to do it for the right reasons. And it can't be in a questionnaire or something like that! You have to be genuinely interested in the other person, but it helps so much with the work that we do, because very few searches go according to plan every time. Either it's not fast enough, or we need more diversity and underrepresented communities, or we're not quite getting the right caliber of talent, or whatever it may be. If you have a good level of understanding, and you have a relationship that you've built over time with the right trust and humility, it ends up being more "we" than "you and me," or "you versus me." You're a peer of that client, and it doesn't matter what it says on their business card and what it says on yours, and how much they're being paid and how much you're being paid. You're the subject matter expert when it comes to recruiting. Unfortunately, it is often the case that, if you haven't earned the right to have those conversations and earned the right for them to listen when you speak, then they will take over and direct you. The client then assumes the role of the subject matter expert in recruiting. Instead, they have to know you to give you that space and the opportunity to speak, and the only way they're going to know you is if you take an interest. Getting to know the external profile is important, but getting to know who they are, the internal being, is the only way.

Part of my role is to help make connections between internal executives. In some companies, those that work in one side of the business just don't know those that are having the biggest impact in another side of the business, because of the speed at which the operation runs. Though we don't own it, I feel we have a huge part to play in connecting those individuals when I feel that it would be important or powerful, or useful for them to have a connection with another executive. I love it when somebody does it for me. Quite often we are blinded – we have great conversations, but it's all centered around requisitions or search work. But over time making these connections becomes more and more important.

—**Roopesh Panchasra, Global Head of Executive Talent Acquisition, Uber**

3. Be genuinely interested, passionate, and enthusiastic.

What's the best way to make that connection? What methods do you use to build good client relationships? It all starts with your first interaction with potential clients. Recognize what is genuine interest in your client and in their businesses versus paying attention to what your client says about their business. As noted above, how often do you call a client to "check in" even when they are not currently seeking your help? There's no purpose to this, no gain for you. However, clients are most interested to hear from you when you are genuinely interested to hear from them about how their business is going, good or bad. Being genuinely interested in someone's business means being with them through both the lows and the highs. Authentic care for the outcome and success of your client's business is what needs to come through in all your conversations, all your reaching out, and in any general interactions.

It is critical for advisors to ask leaders lots of questions to discover and understand their most significant goals. One method is to investigate the client's vision for the long-term, mid-range, and short-term future visions of how their lives would appear if they had accomplished all they desired at the initial meeting, and then to prioritize the significance of their objectives. What is your point of view on what you have found?

While your connection with your client is primarily professional, expressing that you consider them, and the work you do with them, as more than just a job may go a long way. Based on industry, client type, and the personality of the specific client, the amount to which this personal relationship is suitable will vary.

A good leader is enthused about their work or cause, as well as their leadership role. People will be more open to someone who is passionate and dedicated. Recruitment leaders must be able to inspire and motivate candidates around the client's objectives, as they are a natural extension of the organization they are representing in the market. Also, the story a recruiter paints to a candidate must be consistent with what the placed candidate finds starting the role on day one.

To be successful and motivate candidates and clients to take action, you must believe in what you are representing—otherwise it will be glaringly obvious to those around you that you don't. Clients will also be just as interested in your passion as they are in your knowledge. Even if you think you know just about everything about leadership and business, you will still come across as a mediocre advisor if you do not possess confidence and enthusiasm.

LEADERS' WISDOM:
WORK HARD TO UNDERSTAND THE BUSINESS AND
PASSION WILL SHOW THROUGH

● ● ●

As a trusted advisor, the ideal is that you're seen as a true business partner, to be able to bring value into the business with your consulting skills. How you develop those is by having knowledge and understanding of your client's business and challenges. Though we don't have specialists on our team, I say to them that although we're expected to deliver service across the whole enterprise, they should pick two or three functions that they've got a genuine interest in and learn about those functions.

If you can, sit in the town hall and leadership meetings, get a feel for it, the pulse of what's happening internally in terms of the business and the initiatives. Also, look at your competitors: There's a lot of public domain data to look at organizational changes, leadership moves, etc., so get examples of what you learn and bring them to meetings, because while you may think that executives know what's going on at your competitors from a leadership talent or organizational perspective, a majority of the time they don't.

The journey to trusted advisor also hinges on your credibility and your ability to understand. So, when you're asking questions, those questions have meaning in relation to both internal challenges and what's going on externally. I think that it's key to bridge that gap. Now, you can't be an expert on everything, so it's about choosing the disciplines in which you have interests. When you're having discussions with candidates and clients, you'll be using that language and that interest, enthusiasm, and passion will show through.

When talking about credibility, the deal is to under-promise and overdeliver—the usual adage. And I always advise my inexperienced team members that, although they're really keen to make an impact, the best advice I give to them is never promise anything without consideration. Your emotions and your personality will say yes because you want to please the client, but it's better to keep a very measured approach. Listen, ask the right questions, understand all about the role, write notes, then cool off for 24 to 48 hours and then present a written strategy and timeline. It actually gives you a bit of time to research what's going on and then present your strategy based on market data. I also recommend to my team that they talk about themselves and their background when introducing themselves to executive. If you've got 15 years in recruitment, or you specialized in marketing for years, or you placed all of these people in the organization, why not tell the client? How's that not relevant? It also allows to build a more authentic (and hopefully) less transactional relationship. When a search firm consultant comes in for a meeting, it's what they do, and it builds trust and credibility – so why wouldn't an internal consultant do it?

—Mark Tomlinson, Head of Global Executive Recruitment, SC Johnson

4. Be curious: Understand the client's underlying interests and problems to solve.

Trusted advisors work hard to understand the client's underlying interests, not just surface wants. Seek to understand, and then to be understood. It's vital for trusted advisors to take the time to dig below the surface. Try to really understand why clients are asking you to do this specific recruitment work and in a certain way. What's motivating them to do that? What is causing clients to approach things in a particular way on certain matters? Be curious: Ask questions to learn more and form your own point of view to support the client.

As we discussed earlier, it is very important here to practice the "why," not just the "what." Dig deeper and understand the business more and distinguish yourself by learning about the executive leader's or client's corner of the world. Be prepared and informed for the conversation with every executive you meet with. Differentiate yourself from others by assessing needs in detail. Meet with clients on a regular basis to strengthen your understanding of the group's goals, issues, current team talents, and hiring misfires and causes. Perhaps bring along some recent data you've picked up in other candidate conversations. Advisors may deepen their clients' trust by determining and understanding what their clients appreciate the most from them. Focusing on and prioritizing goals (rather than addressing the technical aspects of the recruitment approach) is what many clients value the most. And the most effective method to offering the greatest value to your present (and potential) clients will be to effectively explain to them that you are all on the same page and that you have the required knowledge and skills to assist them reach their goals.

5. Be reliable.

Trusted advisors are reliable: They do what they say they'll do. Say what you're going to do, and then do what you say you're going to do. Deliver—and ideally, overdeliver—on promises, even the small ones.

We all like to believe that we are trustworthy and accountable. Becoming reliable, on the other hand, needs practice and attention. Imagine a world in which every one of your friends, teammates, family members, educators, coaches, and others you interact with on a regular basis accepts complete responsibility for their actions: If everyone you encountered in this hypothetical universe did exactly what they claimed they would do and if people also approached interpersonal relations with the purpose of considering the team's or community's interests in addition to their own.

Chances are, you won't be able to imagine it. The problem is that many people do not uphold their word, even if they are well-intentioned. Taking responsibility for your actions (which includes pledges and obligations) or the expectation of your taking action, as well as the repercussions of that action or inactivity, is the core meaning of accountability. As recruiters and in other walks of life, failure to keep our promises sends a message to others that we are untrustworthy and unpredictable. Now, we recognize that we are all human and humans make mistakes. However, we describe the scenario as a "credibility bank balance." What that means is, as long as you make sure there is a significant positive balance of credibility in the "bank," then you might make a couple of minor withdrawals when you slip up and can't deliver something exactly on time, but the key is to keep that bank balance overwhelmingly in the positive.

Becoming a trusted advisor necessitates a level of personal responsibility that includes creating, maintaining, and accounting for personal commitments. Put simply, when you hold yourself accountable, people around you know you can be relied on to fulfill your obligations or keep your promises. Even the tiny promises count! You get credibility when you follow through on what you claim you'll do—and if you can't do it, then be sure to communicate that ahead of a due date. You gain trust by keeping your word. Holding yourself accountable allows you to be honest, gutsy, motivating, and devoted. Clients and colleagues alike have every right to expect you to be a person who values responsibility as an advisor.

6. Be credible.

Much of your trustworthiness revolves around your credibility. In fact, the two terms are often used interchangeably. Nonetheless, it's still good to point out that trustworthiness refers to how true and factual your statements are, or whether you stand by what you say you'll do or not. On the other hand, credibility is about reputation. It determines your ability to be believed by other people. In simpler terms, it's about how they perceive your trustworthiness.

A good way to establish credibility is to invest in it. Naturally, the tone will be set by your qualifications, experience, and credentials. When people realize they're working with someone who has the expertise and experience to help them through the issues they're facing in their business, they feel more at ease. Nowadays, a "talent advisor" can be found on practically every street corner. Some have gone to school for this; others have not. Some have a solid business history;

others do not. Some people are qualified to perform what they do; others are not. You want to be the successful and trusted advisor who has, who does, and who is!

Strive for honesty and sincerity in whatever you do. Your clients must believe that you truly understand what they are going through, that you are sincere, and that you are, as we previously stated, there for them. Prepare to walk with your clients to empathetically help them in attaining what they may otherwise consider impossible. They should never get the impression that you're only in it for how the outcome will look on your expertise.

LEADERS' WISDOM:
INVESTING TIME IN THE CLIENT'S BUSINESS
CREATES GREATER STRATEGIC VALUE

● ● ●

In my prior company, I was asked to support the manufacturing group but I didn't have the manufacturing experience and didn't know the lingo. I met the leader for the first time and had the conversation: "I don't really know your space, but I really want to, and I can do this by attending your staff meetings and leadership meetings, so I can represent you to candidates on what are those issues that are currently happening, the strategic directional changes you're looking to make, and so on." He was receptive to the idea, so I joined his staff meetings, and it allowed me to actually represent him, talk about the day-to-day operational challenges within the company on a global basis, and talk about the regional impact of that global strategy to those candidates that I was now talking to. There are two nice things that came out of that: First, a level of confidence that I knew what I was speaking about and the credibility in front of candidates where we were just really speaking the right lingo. And, second, as I got into presenting candidates and talking about backgrounds with the business leader, he started to have trust in me and agree with my top candidate recommendations. In fact, there were a couple of times when the client asked me to stand in for him and be part of the interview team review meeting to make sure that everything's on the right path with the interviewers. It got to the point where there was a level of trust where I can go out on the limb and introduce some candidate backgrounds that he wouldn't normally have been interested in, that were outside of what he would normally want. He trusted that they would be strong applicants—and in fact, we actually hired some folks that he initially said he wasn't interested in. Also, after a time, I became proactive with identifying candidates, because I was still in staff meetings and understanding where gaps in talent lie. Not just reacting to openings, but looking at the future needs of this organization.

—**Paul Warner, Director, Executive Recruiting, Physician Recruiting, and System Onboarding, Henry Ford Health System**

7. Be personal.

We all enjoy being reminded that someone cares about us; it makes us feel important and cherished. When you give your clients whatever they want to hear or make promises you can't keep, you're not doing them any favors. You won't have all the answers to every query, but if you're honest and open with your clients at all times, you'll earn their trust. It's also important to remember that saying no is perfectly acceptable. You won't be able to remedy every problem they bring up, but your candor in this area will go a long way.

Advisors should concentrate on the activities that are most critical for attaining clients' objectives, providing value to clients, and strengthening client relationships. Advisors may also help optimize clients' priorities and focus their attention and actions on the main efforts to accomplish those objectives by translating an awareness of the client's personal situation, objectives, and ambitions into an approved detailed strategy.

LEADERS' WISDOM:
BE PROACTIVE WITH YOUR CLIENTS –
STEP INTO DIFFICULT CONVERSATIONS

• • •

One of the keys to what I think has been successful for me in the corporate environment is that I treat my stakeholders as if they're my client and I treat them like I'm an external search firm. So, having that humility, advisory partnership type of relationship I think is really key. I also think it's really important to stay one step ahead of your stakeholders—your "clients"—so that they aren't coming to you to complain about the search. I always felt that way when I was in a search firm too: You need to be one step ahead of them, including in the bad times. For instance, if you know that you're going to have a bad weekly update call, you prepare in advance for that and you are always really direct and communicate clearly that, for instance, this candidate declined our offer so we need to restrategize, or whatever it is. So many people's instincts are to run away and put their head in the sand because they're scared of the repercussions, but I think it's so important to address it head-on and reach out to the client proactively. You need to say, "We're at a restart" or "We're not getting the traction we need." I think it's really important to be proactive with your stakeholders. Not only does it help defuse the situation, but if they feel that you care and that you're doing everything possible to turn things around, it really helps the relationship, and it helps move the search forward.

I think it's also really important that when you go into that bad situation, you go in with either a solution to drive the search in a new direction or ideas to open up the field. We'll have a strategy session with the stakeholders saying: "This isn't working, so how can we expand the search? Are you open to exploring XYZ industry? Can you open up the geographic limitations? Are you open to a slightly different background or work trajectory?" It's really important that you don't just come in and shell out the bad news, but that you have a strategy for a go-forward plan. Maybe they don't agree with the strategy, but at least it gets the conversation started and you get the stakeholder thinking. And if you approach it as, "Let's restrategize the direction of this search," and make them your partner in the solution, it usually helps to defuse the situation. You can't just put it in their lap – you're the search expert, so you have to come up with some creative ideas on how to solve the problem.

—Meg Staunton, Head of Global Executive and Corporate Recruiting, XPO Logistics

8. Be empathetic.

We all understand the importance of empathy in leadership, but do we all have clear knowledge of what empathy is? Some confuse empathy with sympathy; sympathy involves understanding from your own perspective, when you share the feelings of another. Empathy, on the other hand, refers to the ability to recognize or understand the feelings of another. It indicates that you're conscious of their sentiments and how these sentiments influence the other's view. Empathy does not imply that you agree with their point of view; rather, it implies that you are ready and able to understand what the other person is going through.

At first look, this may appear altruistic, but there are real benefits to taking the time to learn what people around us need rather than what we believe is essential. Indeed, advisors who take the time to examine their clients' requirements may offer them the assistance they need to go forward and overcome the problems or obstacles that are preventing them from accomplishing their objectives.

Advisors may establish a sense of trust with their clients by understanding and supplying them with what they need to succeed, therefore enhancing their connections with them and, as a result, people's connections with one another, resulting in increased cooperation and productivity.

A senior-level recruiter is to a large degree a team leader; they are in charge of making sure that a solution is found to the business problem by finding an executive who takes a role that is responsible for solving the problem. In this context, the client is also considered part of the recruiter's team and therefore needs to be advised on how to drive an outcome. One of the roles of leadership is to define the project's vision and set some short-term goals for teams to achieve in order to make your ideas a reality. What separates ordinary to poor leaders from those who thrive in leading others, however, is how the latter recognize that their attention should not be just on whether or not goals are met. Rather, they are focused on achieving the common goal of producing something important.

To do so, leaders (which, in this case, is you as the recruiting expert) must first understand the underlying motivations that drive each of their team members and then connect those motivations with the organization's objectives. This necessitates leaders being more transparent about their ideas and thinking, as well as asking for their input. Recruitment leaders may set the tone and attitude taken by their client to achieve their organization's goals by spending more time learning about their requirements and the motivations behind it.

LEADERS' WISDOM:
BRING YOUR PERSONALITY TO THE PARTY

● ● ●

In my experience, when I dialed up more of me, my client relationships became more authentic, comfortable, and rewarding. In any relationship, including professional ones, you need to bring your personality to the party. Ultimately, people want to work with people they like and they need to get to know the real you, not simply the "consultant" you. Be tenacious, authentic, and empathetic and try to see the world from the other person's perspective. Combine these attributes and, in my mind, you will be giving yourself the very best chance of success.

—**Peter Cave-Gibbs, Consultant, Spencer Stuart**

---

9. Be honest.

"Honesty is the best policy," as they say, and though it shouldn't have to be repeated, it sometimes needs to be. We all use small falsehoods from time to time to protect others or escape conflict. But when you do so, and the other person learns that you spoke less than the truth, if only in the slightest degree, they immediately believe that you might do that about everything. Your prospects of retaining the trust and confidence you've earned will be ruined by even the most minor of deceptions.

While you may want to deliver facts in a palatable manner, what you say should always be rooted in the truth. Whatever message you send to others, they will have to interpret it for themselves. There aren't many messages you can offer that don't have several interpretations. The same may be said of your behavior: People don't always comprehend what you're doing; they have to interpret it for themselves.

You might be wondering how these items relate to trust. The simple answer to that is: In every way. If you've been discovered bending or altering the truth, no matter how slightly, your credibility will be tarnished. This has an impact on how the other person perceives your words and behavior now and in the future, and confirmation bias means they may look for and find other areas to reinforce their belief that you are untrustworthy, whether valid or not. They are more inclined to take a negative view of everything you do if they have doubts about your honesty. This erodes trust even further. We can't stress this enough: One minor untruth may undo all your hard work in creating trust.

LEADERS' WISDOM:
STAY TRUE TO YOURSELF AND GIVE THE
TOUGH MESSAGES WHEN NECESSARY

• • •

The hallmark of a good TA leader is staying true to oneself and providing the right, though at times tough, message to the hiring manager or business. In one instance, we were hiring a regional business leader in Asia. The hiring manager was a newly promoted VP with a reputation for leading tough businesses. The feedback from the candidates was that their interview experience was not that satisfactory, and the hiring manager asked questions that they felt were out of line. We investigated it and found that the hiring manager was not aware of the cultural sensitivities and at times may have accidentally asked candidates to disclose confidential information. We went back to the drawing board to chart some considerations for him to keep in mind while interviewing candidates, encouraged him to balance assessment with "positioning the role appropriately," and helped him structure his business scenarios (with the help of the legal team) to ensure that we didn't cross the line. As we concluded the recruiting process, he appreciated the work done by the team to support him in setting up the guardrails and help him assimilate with the cultural sensitivities.

—Basant Pandey, Director, Global Executive Recruiting, The Goodyear Tire and Rubber Company

10. Be authentic.

Being authentic means acting in ways that reflect your actual personality and feelings. Rather than presenting simply one side of yourself to others, you sincerely exhibit your entire self. That is to say, to be authentic, you must first understand who your inner self is. This necessitates self-awareness and self-acceptance.

We are continually balancing our inner and exterior identities to fit in better and achieve greater success. We are compelled to find "our place" in society and to be valued for who we are and what we have to offer. Many of us are driven even farther, yearning to understand and embody our purpose, to discover deeper meaning in our lives, and to experience the pleasure that comes with becoming a more upstanding person.

Authenticity and purpose are inextricably linked: A strong sense of purpose may assist you in expressing your authenticity, and developing it may frequently assist you in discovering your purpose. You may find the strength of your convictions that moves you profoundly – enough to propel you to advocate for a certain type of beneficial change. In this case, the particular objective may be that of becoming a trusted advisor.

When you express yourself genuinely, you demonstrate to people that you are accountable, that you can be trusted, and that you trust them enough to display your actual, vulnerable self. And people's reactions are frequently positive, making it simpler for you to be you.

Avoid deception and fakery, since people can smell it a mile away. To reiterate, spend time getting to know your clients. Learn about them, their objectives, their families, their interests, and so on. Allow them to get a better sense of who you are as a person by engaging in real conversations on things other than business. People like working with people they like.

As a recruiter, it's your role to refocus and establish or return to a relationship with the function you support in a consultative, value-added way. This starts with the relationship between you and the hiring team. Cement your partnership role through quality focus— have an intimate knowledge of talent together with the right strategy to attract and engage. This set of skills is as valuable as any other in any organization. As a coach and counsel to executive leaders, use data, anecdotal input, your own experiences, and strong business cases for change. In that role, you must be yourself, not a version of who you think the client wants to see. You help strengthen your role as a trusted and valued partner by delivering in this way.

For further reading, we recommend:

The Trusted Advisor, by David Maister, Charles H. Green, and Robert M. Galford (Touchstone, 2001)

The Trusted Advisor Fieldbook: A Comprehensive Toolkit for Leading with Trust, by Charles H. Green and Andrea P. Howe (Wiley, 2011)

TOOLS & FRAMEWORKS

• • •

Visit LeadershipRecruiting.com/tools to download these resources.

KEY ELEMENTS: TIMELINE AND HIRING TEAM KEY ROLES

Key Elements		Define Position, Conduct Internal Search	Begin External Search	Select Search Team	Source, Calibrate, and Present Candidates	Interview Candidates	Extend Offer	Facilitate Onboarding
		• Clarify the business need • Write role description • Build internal candidate slate • Interview internal candidates • Determine if external search is needed	• External search kickoff • Commit to SLA • Develop search strategy • Finalize role description • Select interview team	• Select and engage search team (in-house or external search firm)	• Identify and source candidates • Assess and present calibrated candidates	• Schedule candidate interviews • Provide feedback to candidate and search partner • Make final hiring decision	• Develop and extend the offer	• Develop and implement an on-boarding plan
Timeline			Weeks 1-2	Weeks 3-5	Weeks 6-12	Weeks 8-14	Weeks 15-18	Onboard: Weeks 18-28
Hiring Team Key Roles	Hiring Manager (HM)	• Notify HRGen of exec hiring need • Define business need • Determine level • Draft role description • Review internal candidates • Provide input on search strategy	• Finalize role description • Review and commit to SLA • Select and engage interview team and exec sponsor • Sign off on search strategy	• Participate in external search firm selection process, if appropriate	• Provide input on sourced candidates • Refine search specifications • Participate in update calls with search team • Provide feedback on candidates presented	• Brief hiring team • Interview candidates • Provide detailed feedback • Select final candidate • Own selling candidate • If no candidate selected, reevaluate search • If re-start, redefine role description	• Approve final offer • Drive PR plan	• Ensure new hire set up and onboarding plan • New hire announcement to team
	HR Generalist (HR Gen)	• Hold position clarification meeting • Review business need with HM • Help determine level • Help write role description • Develop slate of internal candidates • Develop internal search strategy • Complete staffing requisition • Secure appropriate approvals	NA	NA	NA	• Interview candidates if appropriate • Provide feedback • Assist in selection of final candidate • If no candidate selected, reevaluate search with HM • If re-start, help HM redefine role description	• Advise on candidate offer • Input on PR release plan	• Ensure new hire setup • Works with leadership development person to facilitate onboarding plan
	Executive Recruiter (ER)	NA	• Conduct search kickoff meeting • Determine whether external search partner is needed • Present sample profiles for calibration, if available • Edit/finalize role description • Meet with interview team (if approp.) • Develop and finalize search strategy	• Research and select search firm or choose internal search team • Engage and contract with firm • Set expectations for deliverables, timing, and communications	*If no search firm engaged:* • Research and source candidates • Conduct candidate assessments • Present qualified, screened candidates. • Provide regular updates to HM (ideally at least every two weeks) *If search firm engaged:* • Schedule weekly updates with search firm • Provide ongoing liaison between search partner and HM	• Manage candidate scheduling (agenda, travel, accommodations) • Host candidate for interviews • Send morning mail and facilitate IV process • Provide feedback on candidate to search team and search partner • Drive the candidate "courting and sell" strategy • Give candidate interview feedback (if no search partner) • If no candidate selected, reevaluate search and redefine role description with HM and HR Gen	• Gather detailed compensation information • Devise offer recommendation in partnership with Compensation Org. • Extend offer and negotiate • Provide information for PR release	• Provide input to on-boarding plan • Escort hire to new employee orientation • Ensure hand off to leadership development partner and HRGen
	External Search Partner (Retained search firm)	NA	NA	• Selected search partner(s) present credentials and pitch their firm	• Meet with HM (if approp.) • Tweak final role description • Research and source candidates • Conduct candidate interviews • Write detailed candidate assessments • Document progress to ER • Participate in regular update calls	• Prepare candidate for interviews • Provide candidate with post-interview feedback • If no candidate selected, redefine role description with HM and ER as necessary	• Gather detailed compensation information • Provide input on final offer	• Follow up with new hire prior to start date
	OD/ Leadership Development Consultant	• Research internal candidates	• Review and provide input to final role description, if possible	NA	NA	NA	NA	• Develop and implement new hire on-boarding plan • Provide followup and coaching to new hire
	Compensation	• Provide input on industry payscale for level	NA	NA	NA	NA	• Develop final offer in partnership with Exec Recruiter	NA
	Interview Team (Exec Sponsor and Search Committee)	NA	• Review and provide input to final role description • Conduct meetings with ER	NA	NA	• Interview candidates • Provide feedback • Assist in selling candidate	NA	• Support effective on-boarding of new hire

THE EXECUTIVE SEARCH PROCESS CHECKLIST

Clarify the Need and Develop a Strategy

_____ Identify and validate the need. Is it clear? Are there internal candidates?

_____ Establish hiring team and brief them on the process.

_____ Develop initial role description:
Primary responsibilities and reporting relationships
How the role may evolve

_____ Develop initial compensation target.

_____ Search directly or use a search firm?

_____ Any issues of confidentiality?

_____ Local candidates or relocation?

Select a Search Partner (if using one)

_____ Identify external search consultants with relevant track records.

_____ Solicit information to document capabilities.

_____ Check references.

_____ Meet with the two or three most qualified consultants.

_____ Discuss where and how candidates will be identified.

_____ Discuss potential conflicts and obstacles.

_____ Seek fee bids and acceptance of engagement terms.

_____ Establish time frame for each step in the search.

Begin the Search

_____ Meet with external search consultant or in-house recruiter to discuss the role in depth.

_____ Collectively agree on the role description.

_____ Identify known potential candidates and referral sources.

_____ Schedule likely candidate interview dates for the hiring team.

Calibrate Candidates

_____ Meet with recruiter to discuss the long list.

_____ Review implications: Adjust role description? Access new candidate pools?

_____ Conduct weekly phone updates on candidate development.

Interview Candidates

_____ Full briefing for hiring team before each candidate interview.

_____ Structured interviews with immediate, detailed feedback.

_____ Identify and pursue finalists.

_____ Second interviews, further assessment.

_____ Additional reference checking and background verification.

Extend an Offer

_____ Develop the offer and preview it to the selected candidate.

_____ Extend the offer.

Facilitate Onboarding

_____ Develop onboarding plan.

_____ Process new-hire paperwork.

_____ Hand off to leadership development group.

_____ Follow up regularly.

EXECUTIVE RECRUITMENT SERVICE-LEVEL AGREEMENT

Position Title:	Hiring Manager:
Position Level:	Executive Recruiter:
Date Initiated:	Recruiting Team:

A successful search is typically a result of a close partnership between the hiring manager (HM) and executive recruiter (ER), where both parties are clear on responsibilities and execute crisply on their commitments. This service-level agreement (SLA) outlines ownership for each area of responsibility and will serve as the road map to guide the process and dictate deliverables.

Role	Responsibilities
Hiring Manager (HM)	• Ultimately responsible for hiring decision • Clarify need for position and level • Complete role description • Review and commit to SLA • Accommodate regular search status meetings • Recommend candidate leads or events where candidate might be available; solicit the same from team • Identify and brief interview team and executive sponsor • Assign focus areas for each interviewer • Provide feedback on candidates presented within 48 hours of receipt or otherwise negotiated • Reserve time for candidate interviews • Help "court and sell" candidate during interviews • Provide prompt and detailed interview feedback • Revisit and redefine position requirements throughout the search, if necessary • Approve final offer • Engage with candidate after offer is extended to help close • Drive public relations plan, new hire setup, and onboarding program • Participate in postmortem meeting with ER

Role	Responsibilities
Executive Recruiter (ER)	• Lead search kickoff meeting • Oversee development and approval of role description • Establish search strategy: • Choose external search partner or internal team • Direct research and sourcing of candidates • Present target list and sample profiles • Establish "courting and selling" strategy • Source and screen candidates • Manage interview process: • Present candidates to HM (résumé and assessment) with recommendations based on position profile, candidate profile, and business requirements • Oversee candidate interview scheduling • Host candidate for interviews • Drive communications: • Conduct status meetings with HM (ideally weekly and at minimum every two weeks) • Issue "morning mail" with assigned focus areas • Collect interview feedback • Provide hire/no-hire recommendation • Provide candidate with feedback • Manage offer process: • Collect current compensation data on candidate • Work with compensation to drive offer recommendation • Secure offer approval from Human Resources and HM • Extend offer to candidate (verbal and written) • Brief hiring manager for follow-up • Manage post-offer negotiations • Trigger relocation process • Greet hire on first day • Confirm onboarding activities • Conduct postmortem meeting with HM

SPECIFICS

The search will commence upon (1) agreement to these terms and (2) completion of the role description, which will be completed by the HM by _____ .

- ER and HM agree to meet for status updates every _____ weeks.
- HM agrees to commit _____ hours per month to review/assess/interview candidates.
- Search strategy will be completed by _____ .
- Hiring manager will engage interview team and exec sponsor by _____ .
- Estimated search completion date is _____ .

HOLD/TERMINATION

The HM or ER may terminate the search at any time, with prompt notification and detailed reason. Examples include:

- More than six qualified candidates interviewed with no hire or no decision
- Candidates assessed and rejected based on requirements outside the position specification
- HM or ER not fully engaged on the search (e.g., unresponsive, unable to meet regularly)
- Altered needs based on changes in group structure from reorganization, termination, promotion, etc.

SEARCH POSTMORTEM

A postmortem will be conducted at the conclusion of the search, at which time we will review and discuss the process, candidate slate, time frame, and partnership to identify those areas where improvements could have been made. This will help to ensure an excellent experience for future candidates and preserve the company's reputation for having a professional and respectful hiring process.

REFERENCES
• • •

Allcorn, S. (2006). Psychoanalytically informed executive coaching. In D. R. Stober & A. M. Grant (Eds.), Evidence based coaching handbook. Hoboken, NJ: John Wiley & Sons.

Arnold, J. (2011). The impact of coaching in the workplace. http://coach4executives.com/coaching/the-impact-of-coaching-in-the-workplace/.

Auerbach, J. E. (2006). Cognitive coaching. In D. R. Stober & A. M. Grant (Eds.), Evidence based coaching handbook. Hoboken, NJ: John Wiley & Sons.

Berger, J. G. (2006). Adult development theory and executive coaching practice. In D. R. Stober & A. M. Grant (Eds.), Evidence based coaching handbook. Hoboken, NJ: John Wiley & Sons.

Biech, E. (2003). Marketing your consulting services. San Francisco: Pfeiffer. Chapter 1 (pgs. 1–16).

Binning, J. F., & Barrett, G. V. (1989). Validity of personnel decisions: A conceptual analysis of the inferential and evidential bases. *Journal of Applied Psychology* 74, 478–494.

Block, P. (2011). Flawless consulting: A guide to getting your expertise used (3rd ed.). San Francisco: Pfeiffer. http://www.eblib.com.

Bulgarella, C. (2018). Purpose-driven companies evolve faster than others. https://www.forbes.com/sites/caterinabulgarella/2018/09/21/purpose-driven-companies-evolve-faster-than-others/?sh=7ebf9d5655bc.

Cascio, W. F., & Aguinis, H. (2011). Applied psychology in human management (7th ed.). Upper Saddle River, NJ: Prentice Hall.

Cashman, K. (2008). Leadership from the inside out: Becoming a leader for life (2nd ed., rev. and expanded). San Francisco: Berrett-Koehler.

Cashman, K. (2017). The four levers for enduring leadership purpose. forbes.com/sites/kevincashman/2017/09/05/a-true-measure-of-leadership-success-sevenguiding-principles.

Cashman, K. (2017). How to help your senior team rediscover its core purpose. https://chiefexecutive.net/help-senior-team-rediscover-core-purpose/.

Caulkin, S. (2016). Companies with a purpose beyond profit tend to make more money. https://www.ft.com/content/b22933e0-b618-11e5-b147-e5e5bba42e51.

Clutterbuck, D. (2010). Coaching reflection: The liberated coach. *Coaching* 3(1), 73–81.

Coleman, A. M. (2015). A dictionary of psychology (4th ed.). Oxford: Oxford University Press.

Collins, J. (2001). Good to Great. New York: HarperCollins.

Creel, P. (2018). Think like a gardener and cultivate a thriving business culture. https://www.linkedin.com/pulse/think-like-gardener-cultivate-thriving-business-culture-creel-price/.

Davis, S. L., & McKenna, D. D. (2002). Activating the active ingredients of leadership coaching. In G. Hernez-Broome & L. A. Boyce (Eds.), Advancing executive coaching: Setting the course for successful leadership coaching. San Francisco: Jossey-Bass.

Davis, S. L., & Barnett, R. C. (2010). Changing behavior one leader at a time. In R. Silzer & B. E. Dowell (Eds.), Strategy-driven talent management: A leadership imperative. San Francisco: Jossey-Bass.

Davidson, J. (2002). The discipline of evaluation: A helicopter tour for I-O psychologists. *Industrial-Organizational Psychologist* 40 (2), 31–35.

Desrosiers, E., & Oliver, D. H. (2011). Maximizing impact: Creating successful partnerships between coaches and organizations (links to an external site.) In G. Hernez-Broome and L. A. Boyce (Eds.), Advancing executive coaching: setting the course for successful leadership coaching. San Francisco: Jossey-Bass.

Farr, J. L., & Tippins, N. T. (Eds.). (2013). Handbook of employee selection. London: Routledge. http://www.ebrary.com.

Fitzgerald, C., & Garvey Berger, J. (2002). Executive coaching: Practices and perspectives (1st ed.). Mountain View, CA: Davies-Black Publishing.

Gatewood, R. D., Feild, H. S., & Barrick, M. (2016). Human resource selection (8th ed.). Mason, OH: Cengage.

Gino, F. (2018). The business case for curiosity. https://hbr.org/2018/09/the-business-case-for-curiosity.

Goleman, D. , McKee, A., & Boyatsis, R. (2002). Primal leadership: Realizing the power of emotional intelligence. Boston: Harvard Business School Press.

Green, C.H., & Howe, A. P. (2011). The trusted advisor fieldbook: A comprehensive toolkit for leading with trust. Hoboken, NJ: Wiley.

Gregory, A. (2010). 4 elements of trust needed for successful collaboration. https://www.sitepoint.com/4-elements-of-trust-for-collaboration/.

Gurdjian, P., Halbeisen, T., & Lane, K. (2014). Why leadership development programs fail. http://www.mckinsey.com/global-themes/leadership/why-leadership-development-programs-fail.

Hicks, B., Carter. A., & Sinclair, A. (2013). Impact of coaching on employee well-being, engagement, and job satisfaction. http://www.employment-studies.co.uk/system/files/resources/files/hrp8.pdf.

Hodgetts, W. H. (2002). Using executive coaching in organizations: What can go wrong (and how to prevent it). In C. Fitzgerald & J. Garvey Berger (Eds.), Executive coaching: Practices and perspectives. Mountain View, CA: Davies-Black Publishing.

Kenny, G. (2014). Your company's purpose is not its vision, mission or values. https://hbr.org/2014/09/your-companys-purpose-is-not-its-vision-mission-or-values.

Kubr, M. (2005). Management consulting: A guide to the profession (4th ed.). Washington, DC: International Labor Office.

Kurpius, D. J., Fuqua, D. R., & Rozecki, T. (1993). The consulting process: A multidimensional approach. *Journal of Counseling and Development* 71(6), 601–606.

Maister, D., C. H. Green, & R. M. Galford. (2001). The trusted advisor. New York: Touchstone.

McGonagill, G. (2002). The coach as reflective practitioner. In C. Fitzgerald & J. G. Berger (Eds.), Executive coaching: practices and perspectives. Mountain View, CA: Davies-Black Publishing.

McGovern, J., Lindemann, M., Vergara, M., Murphy, S., Barker, L., & Warrenfeltz, R. (2001). Maximizing the impact of executive coaching: Behavioral change, organizational outcomes, and return on investment. *Manchester Review.* https://www.perspect.ca/pdf/ExecutiveCoaching.pdf.

Mullins, S., & Lord, D. (2020). Leadership recruiting: Strategy, tactics and tools for hiring organizations. Bellevue, WA: LDRS Publishing.

Nelson, K., & Hausler, D. (2006). Consulting. In M. M. Helms (Ed.). Encyclopedia of management (5th ed). Detroit: Gale. Pgs. 120–121. https://www.gale.com/.

Peterson, D. B. (2006). People are complex, and the world is messy: A behavior-based approach to executive coaching. In D. R. Stober & A. M. Grant (Eds.), Evidence based coaching handbook. Hoboken, NJ: John Wiley & Sons.

Scott, B. (2000). Consulting on the inside: An internal consultant's guide to living and working inside organizations. American Society of Training and Development. Chapter 14 (p. 189).

SHRM Foundation. (2009). Recruiting and attracting talent: A guide to understanding and managing the recruitment process. Alexandria, VA: SHRM Foundation.

Stober, D. R. (2006). Coaching from a humanistic perspective. In D. R. Stober & A. M. Grant (Eds.), Evidence-based coaching handbook. Hoboken, NJ: John Wiley & Sons.

Stowell, S. (2021). The 5 most common problems of organizations. https://cmoe.com/blog/organizational-problem/.

Ventura, M. (2018). Applied empathy: The new language of leadership. New York: Atria Books.

Verlinden, N. (2021). 7 ways to assess organizational fit. https://harver.com/blog/organizational-fit/.

White, S. (2011). The downside of hiring people just like you. http://www.theglobeandmail.com/report-on-business/small-business/sb-managing/human-resources/the-downside-of-hiring-people-just-like-you/article555612/.

Whitmore, J. (2002). Coaching for performance (3rd ed.). London: Nicholas Brealey.

Zollers, A. (2011). Understanding the nature of resistance. http://johnnyholland.org/2011/05/understanding-the-nature-of-resistance/.

ABOUT THE AUTHORS
• • •

Simon Mullins is the world's leading independent consultant on executive recruiting in organizations of all sizes.

Corporate executive recruiting lives at the intersection of corporate strategy and people. Here, the toughest decisions are made on who will shape the future of the enterprise. It's a critical, narrow field in which Simon's experience runs deep. His reputation is practically synonymous with the topic.

Simon has been a recruiting leader for almost his entire career — he even started a recruiting agency while a student at university. Simon has lived and worked in Europe, Asia, and the United States (on both coasts) from startups to a *Fortune* 50 company.

After beginning his recruiting career in London, Simon moved to Hong Kong to recruit for clients in the technology industry. He managed executive search from "the outside" as a Partner at Korn Ferry. He spent seven years at the firm in Boston and in Silicon Valley.

In 2004, Simon joined Microsoft's Executive Recruiting Team, which he led from 2006 to 2013, eventually becoming Senior Director of the company. The team became highly integrated with Microsoft's succession planning process and was responsible for all external hiring of the company's most impactful executives, including board directors.

In 2013, Simon was asked to become Senior Director of Staffing of Microsoft's largest experienced staffing team, serving the Applications and Services Group.

In 2014 — after serving as an Advisory Board Member from 2007 to 2012 — Simon joined the Executive Search Information Exchange (ESIX). He now leads and facilitates the group. ESIX (esix.org), funded entirely by hiring organizations, is the world's leading independent information source for corporate executive recruiting leaders.

Simon's previous book, coauthored with David Lord, is *Leadership Recruiting: Strategy, Tactics, and Tools for Hiring Organizations* (2020). He is a frequent speaker at industry forums, workshop facilitator, and media commentator.

Simon holds an honors degree in economics and public administration from the University of London.

Find Simon on LinkedIn or write to him at Simon@ESIX.org.

Kelli Vukelic is the Chief Executive Officer of N2Growth where she oversees the firm's executive search and advisory services globally.

N2Growth operates in 50 markets across the Americas, EMEA, and APAC. N2Growth has long been regarded by *Forbes* as a Top 15 executive search firm.

Kelli is an industry veteran, having spent her entire career in executive search. She brings over 24 years of experience to every team and client interaction — melding strategy with executive search, leadership development, and organizational psychology. Her areas of expertise include talent operations, strategy, and C-suite executive recruitment, mainly in technology organizations. Her experience in these areas spans across geographies and organizations of varying sizes. Kelli's passion is purpose-driven leadership, where individuals and organizations can use purpose alignment to drive greater personal fulfillment while accelerating organizational performance.

Prior to assuming her current responsibilities, Kelli served as Chief Operating Officer of N2Growth, leading both business and sales operations while driving the innovations required to establish the future of executive search. Before joining N2Growth, she held several roles of increasing responsibility at Korn Ferry over her 20-year tenure culminating in an executive leadership role in the firm's global technology practice.

Kelli holds a Bachelor of Science in Technology with a focus on Leadership and Management from the British Columbia Institute of Technology. She has also earned a Master of Arts in Industrial and Organizational Psychology from Adler University.

Kelli and her husband have four children and a French bulldog. They reside in West Vancouver, BC, Canada.

Find Kelli on LinkedIn or write to her at k.vukelic@n2growth. com.

ACKNOWLEDGMENTS
• • •

Many hands make light work, and this is definitely true of this book.

In the first instance, it would not have been possible without the love and support of Simon's wife and business partner, Barbara, along with their children Annie, Izzy, and Isaac; and Kelli's husband, Boyan, and their children Sofia, Silas, Sidney, and Emil.

Similarly, we cannot thank enough all the recruiting experts and leaders who have contributed to these pages and to our own education, personal growth, and professional development over the years.

This book also benefits from the invaluable professional assistance of Carolyn Monaco, Monica Jainschigg, Jayme Johnson, Kelly Messier, Barbara Caraballo, and Laura Shelley.

INDEX

• • •

WHY ESIX?

The Executive Search Information Exchange (ESIX) delivers research, tools, training, and peer networking to heads of executive recruiting at leading organizations worldwide. The group has met more than 400 times and includes most of its original members from 1994, plus 100 more organizations from around the world.

Members attend regular meetings in various business centers in the United States, Europe, and Asia. They also attend online events on a variety of topics relevant to the recruitment of senior executives.

Participating organizations are entitled to a menu of benefits, including networking meetings, benchmark surveys, live and on-demand training, and online tools including the execSmart database of search and research consultants.

ESIX is completely independent, 100% member-focused, and

"I have belonged to other orgs that don't go the extra mile as you just did. Thanks again!" —Lena Allison, **Ford Motor Company**

"Great materials!" —Nidhi Hiremath, **BT Group**

"Thanks for keeping us connected during these times." —Jackie Morgan, **Eaton**

"Informative, insightful and delightful." —Eric Goldstein, **SAP**

"Thanks for your work—ESIX has been a great resource for me this year coming into executive recruiting, and I've really appreciated it and grown from it. Looking forward to networking in the new year with everyone." —Stephanie Kempa, **Danaher**

"I have loved partnering with you. You have helped me tremendously in my career." —Toni Unrein, formerly **T-Mobile**

"Truly a fruitful and productive dialogue and information share." —Shannon Pereira, **PepsiCo**

"ESIX membership enabled me to connect with peers to get their help with ways to modernize our executive searches and train my team in a different approach." —Gwendolyn DeFilippi, **US Air Force**

For more, contact Simon@ESIX.org

ALSO AVAILABLE!

In business, recruiting the right leaders at the right time is *the* competitive advantage.

Leadership Recruiting is the authoritative guide you need to find and develop the very best leaders for your organization.

What was once managed by instinct can now be driven by 25 years of research and experience with many of the world's leading organizations.

Get your copy and gain your competitive edge.

By the world's leading independent consultants, Simon Mullins and David Lord, CEO and Founder (respectively) of the Executive Search Information Exchange (ESIX.org).